MW00769935

7/22

The Alien and Sedition Acts of 1798

WITNESS TO HISTORY

Peter Charles Hoffer and Williamjames Hull Hoffer, *Series Editors*

ALSO IN THE SERIES

the alien and sedition acts of 1798

TESTING THE CONSTITUTION

Terri Diane Halperin

Johns Hopkins University Press | Baltimore

© 2016 Johns Hopkins University Press
All rights reserved. Published 2016
Printed in the United States of America on acid-free paper
9 8 7 6 5 4 3 2 1

Johns Hopkins University Press
2715 North Charles Street
Baltimore, Maryland 21218-4363
www.press.jhu.edu

Library of Congress Cataloging-in-Publication Data

Names: Halperin, Terri Diane, 1966– author.
Title: The Alien and Sedition Acts of 1798 : testing the constitution
   / Terri Diane Halperin.
Description: Baltimore : Johns Hopkins University Press, 2016. | Series:
   Witness to history | Includes bibliographical references and index.
Identifiers: LCCN 2015034016| ISBN 9781421419688 (hardback) |
   ISBN 9781421419695 (paperback) | ISBN 9781421419701 (electronic)
Subjects: LCSH: United States. Sedition Act of 1798. | Alien and Sedition
   laws, 1798. | Seditious libel—Law and legislation—United States.—
   History—18th century. | Freedom of expression—United States.—
   History—18th century. | BISAC: HISTORY / United States / General. |
   POLITICAL SCIENCE / Government / General. | LAW / Constitutional.
Classification: LCC KF9397.A3281798 H35 2016 | DDC 324.73/0231—dc23
LC record available at http://lccn.loc.gov/2015034016

A catalog record for this book is available from the British Library.

Special discounts are available for bulk purchases of this book.
For more information, please contact Special Sales at 410-516-6936 or
specialsales@press.jhu.edu.

Johns Hopkins University Press uses environmentally friendly book
materials, including recycled text paper that is composed of at least
30 percent post-consumer waste, whenever possible.

For Alex, Elias, and Lida

Contents

The Alien and Sedition Acts of 1798

prologue

ON THE EVENING of May 7, 1798, a few hundred men intent on inflicting harm upon their political opponents marched through the streets of Philadelphia. They had one particular target in mind—Benjamin Franklin Bache, a printer who in his newspaper, the *Aurora*, routinely, forcefully, and quite nastily criticized President John Adams and his predecessor George Washington. In preparation for the mob, Bache gathered his friends to defend his property. All the young men could do was to hurl threats and insults.

The assault on Bache was not the first event of the night for these men. Earlier in the evening, a larger group of about 1,000 young men visited President Adams's house to pledge their support and to offer their services for the defense of the nation. Only days before, Americans had learned that Adams's diplomatic mission to France, the purpose of which had been to negotiate an end to French attacks on American shipping, had failed spectacularly with what became known as the XYZ Affair. The Quasi-War with France would continue and mostly likely intensify. These men now promised to support Adams's policies in any way they could. On this night, Adams, dressed in full military uniform and with a sword at his side, proudly accepted the young men's accolades by saying, "no prospect or spectacle could excite a stronger sensibility in my bosom than this which now presents itself before me."[1] After visiting the president, the group repaired to dinner, where most certainly numerous toasts to the country, the Union, the Constitution, and its leaders were made. It was after this dinner that the smaller group left for Bache's house. Although Bache fended them off this time, the tumult was far from over.

Two days later, on May 9, violence erupted in the streets. Adams had declared the day to be a fast day, a day for the nation to pray for peace and deliverance from the crisis with France. Defiantly, Bache rejected the fast, going about his business as usual. In the *Aurora* that day, he printed an editorial in which he criticized young men's involvement in politics by declaring, "They have not discretion sufficient to ballast their zeal."[2] Certainly, the men who had paraded through the streets a few days before believed that Bache was insulting them. Another mob formed that night with the intent of burning Bache's house to punish his defiance, but again Bache was able to defend his property. With the help of his friends and neighbors, Bache refused to concede ground to the Federalist mob. A few months later, he published a pamphlet titled "Truth Will Out! The Foul Charges of the Tories against the Editor . . . repelled by positive proof and plain truth and his base calumniators put to shame," detailing the Federalists' efforts to silence him. Bache's choice of title showed that he expected the truth of the Federalists' treachery would come out and lead to their defeat. Of the May 7 attack, he declared, "It will serve only to convince the Editor of the number and spirit of his friends; who shewed themselves . . . determined . . . to assist him in repelling force by force."[3]

While his house may have been safe, the rest of Philadelphia was not, and many residents believed themselves to be in danger. Pennsylvania's governor called out the militia to restore peace in the streets. Reporting on the unrest, Vice President Thomas Jefferson noted that, for the few days preceding the fast, supporters of both the Federalists and Democratic-Republicans took to the streets but not always at the same time or place. On May 9, when both groups were out in force, Jefferson described the scene as "so filled with confusion from about 6. to 10. oclock last night that it was dangerous going out."[4] Fifteen years later, Adams could still recall the terror of that day when he estimated that more than 10,000 people flooded the streets. He certainly believed that his own life was in danger as he praised his servants for being willing to "Sacrifice their Lives in my defence." Even with his servants' protection, Adams "judged it prudent and necessary to order Chests of Arms from the War Office to be brought through bye Lanes and back Doors" to defend his residence.[5] It was not just the streets of Philadelphia that were unsafe—the whole republic seemed at risk.

There was certainly enough blame to go around. Newspapers throughout the country printed at least two versions of those early May events. In one account, Bache's supporters and those wearing tricolored cockades in support of the French Revolution and Democratic-Republican Party were censured for failing to disperse as ordered by the mayor and other officials. Order was only restored when the "cavalry paraded through the city during the night, and a number of young men who voluntarily offered themselves . . . as guards to the military mint, &c." protected the city. The other version accused Federalist newspapers editors—particularly Peter Porcupine, the pen name of the English printer William Cobbett, who was just as much a Federalist as Bache was a Democratic-Republican—for daring young Federalists to take to the streets. Cobbett had predicted tumult, which was exactly what happened. The writer accused "the fabricators of this scheme of arraying our citizens against each other." He predicted that they would only succeed in pushing the nation over the precipice and into a revolution, which the friends of order (as Federalists often called themselves) had desperately sought to avoid.[6]

Such public displays—whether peaceful, boisterous marches through town or violence directed against a particular person or symbol—had long been part of American politics.[7] In the 1790s, Federalists and Democratic-Republicans used public meetings, demonstrations, dinners, toasts, and other methods to explain their views to the people, to prove that they had the people's support, and to garner that support. Of course, neither party was ever in complete control of these demonstrations, and mobs assumed an ambiguous role in American politics. This particular mob was sanctioned by the president when Adams met them in full military regalia and accepted their support. A few days later, the mob's character had changed. It seemed more unruly and dangerous. The public now seemed to disapprove of the mob, making no outcry when the militia was called out to restore the peace. In fact, in many ways the mobs and Bache had acted as expected. When the young men marched to Adams's house and pledged their fidelity to the Union and Adams's policies, they were behaving as Federalists believed the people should. They were showing their support for Adams, the government, and thus the nation. By attacking Bache, the mob confronted someone who seemed intent on damaging and dividing the nation. In contrast, by being a persistent critic of the government and openly disobeying Adams's fast day proclamation, Bache was fulfilling the role Democratic-Republicans prescribed to the people. In this view, the people were to be ever watchful of the government to ensure officials did not violate the people's rights.

Differences over the role of the people in a republic as embodied by Bache and the Philadelphia mobs were one point of separation between the parties, which may better be characterized as coalitions. Often the ties between local, state, and national leaders were loose, and the parties could accommodate a diversity of opinions. The Federalist and Democratic-Republican Parties had developed over the course of the first half of the 1790s after the ratification of the Constitution. These divisions were similar to those factions that emerged during the debate over the ratification of the Constitution between Federalists and Anti-Federalists. Most, but not all, Federalists joined the Federalist Party, and the vast majority of Anti-Federalists became Democratic-Republicans. The initial divisions had occurred over Treasury Secretary Alexander Hamilton's financial program and solidified over conflicts regarding relations with Great Britain and the Jay Treaty of 1795. Throughout the decade, the parties remained largely sectional, with the Federalists strongest in New England and Democratic-Republicans in the South with the exception of South Carolina, which had a Federalist majority. The Middle States were more closely divided. Generally, the Federalists had a more commercial orientation, the Democratic-Republicans a more agrarian one.

The Philadelphia Convention delegates did not plan for political parties when writing the Constitution. The existence of national political parties or coalitions itself was a problem because most Americans associated them with corruption, believing that parties had no constructive role in a republic. Indeed, Americans' persistent anti-partyism was a feature of politics in the 1790s. One constant question was who could and did speak for the people. Federalists would have quickly answered that government officials, chosen by the people, spoke for them and that the people spoke through elections. Democratic-Republicans would have said that the people spoke for themselves. Yet an important question remained: through what means could the people speak? Elected officials, petitions, public meetings, demonstrations, organized groups, newspapers? Federalists wanted to define those means quite narrowly and tried to do so through the Alien and Sedition Acts. Democratic-Republicans sought a broader definition.

The new constitution divided powers and responsibilities between state and national governments and within the new federal government. Within this structure, Americans asked whether the state governments, representatives in Congress, or the president best represented them and protected their interests. Sometimes none of them did; other times people chose the state governments, which could be more attuned to local concerns; and other times people looked to the federal government. Such questions of federalism persist today. In the 1790s, they were at the base of many of the most contentious issues and helped to define the differences between the Federalist and Democratic-Republican Parties.

The disagreements over policy of the first half of the 1790s reflected the parties' distinct visions of the republic. On the one hand, Federalists favored a strong national government, a foreign policy that protected commercial interests, and a domestic policy that proactively encouraged the nation's economic development. Although they would court popular support in limited and controlled ways, they were wary of unfettered popular participation in politics and suspicious of the ideas of democracy, equality, and liberty being touted by European radicals and revolutionaries in the 1790s. This concern was one reason Bache's activities and newspaper created such anxieties for Federalists. On the other hand, Democratic-Republicans tended to favor strong state governments, a foreign policy that favored other republics, and a domestic policy that did not favor one interest over another. Democratic-Republicans believed the people should play an active role in policy making. Although not all people who identified as Democratic-Republicans would embrace the ideas of democracy, liberty, and equality with equal enthusiasm, they did not identify these ideas as threats to the Union. Federalists and Democratic-Republicans did have important points of agreement. They both believed it was best if the United States remained neutral in the European wars in the 1790s, but they disagreed on the terms of that neutrality. They wanted to protect and preserve their republic, but again clashed over which threats posed the greatest dangers and how best to combat those hazards.

One issue dividing Americans was how to both support and disagree with government policies. Bache and the mobs embodied this struggle. Americans argued about how much criticism a young republic could withstand. Some did not see any danger in a vigorous political debate. When violence erupted, these men argued that more democratic debate could alleviate the perceived necessity of violence. Others recoiled from the chaos and uncertainty to argue that a more limited discussion would suffice. The May 1798 mobs and the reaction to them exemplified these different visions of the role of the people and debate in the American Republic.

To combat the chaos of the late 1790s and to quell the violence that political debate produced, the Federalists enacted the Alien and Sedition Acts, a set of four laws, in the summer of 1798. The Naturalization Act increased the residency requirement for citizenship from five to fourteen years. Significantly, it established a federal registry of all aliens and prohibited state courts from naturalizing citizens. Citizenship became exclusively the federal government's responsibility. The Alien Friends Act, which expired in June 1800, gave the president the power to jail and to deport aliens he suspected of dangerous or suspicious activities. The Alien Enemies Act was essentially the same as the Alien Friends Act, but it would only become effective in the event of a formally declared war. Because war with France was never declared, the Alien Enemies Act was not invoked.* Both laws denied immigrants the right to a fair hearing and access to the judicial system. They placed great trust in the president's discretion to act fairly and with cause. Finally, the Sedition Act operated directly against citizens—the only law of the four to do so. Citizens were prohibited from writing or speaking critically of the president, Congress, or government upon penalty of imprisonment and a fine. The law expired on March 3, 1801, the final day of John Adams's term as president.

The effectiveness of the Alien and Sedition Acts cannot simply be measured by the number of deportations or convictions for sedition. While no aliens were deported under the Alien Friends Act, some were watched and many, particularly recent French immigrants, voluntarily left the country or delayed their planned emigration rather than subject themselves to an arbitrary law. Although there were only fourteen indictments under the Sedition Act in addition to the three under common law, all were against Democratic-Republicans; most were against newspaper editors and writers. Federalists targeted those who they thought posed the greatest danger to the nation. Democratic-Republicans had to watch what they said, and many moderated their public comments rather than invite arrest.

A key issue in the debate was the meaning of the Bill of Rights. The ab-

---

* Unlike the Alien Friends and Sedition Acts, the Alien Enemies Act never expired. It was invoked during World War II to arrest and put under surveillance immigrants from Germany, Italy, and Japan.

sence of such a bill of rights had been one of the strongest arguments against ratification of the Constitution in 1787–88. During the First Congress, Virginian James Madison, who had quickly emerged as a leader in the House of Representatives, made good on his promise made during his congressional campaign against James Monroe to remedy this weakness. The Constitution's first ten amendments provided important protections to individuals that the Alien and Sedition Acts denied. The Fifth and Sixth Amendments guarantee the right to due process and a fair and speedy trial, but the Alien Acts denied immigrants these rights. The First Amendment prohibits Congress from passing laws "respecting an establishment of religion, or prohibiting the free exercise thereof; or abridging the freedom of speech, or of the press; or the right of the people peaceably to assemble, and to petition the Government for a redress of grievances." The Sedition Act infringed upon the rights of speech, but, as many opponents argued, the law also posed a threat to the other rights listed in the amendment—particularly the rights to petition and assembly and ultimately the right to free elections. Many Anti-Federalists had believed that the amendments were merely "throwing a tub to the whale," simply creating a distraction, much as when seamen would throw an empty tub toward a whale for him to play with rather than ram their ship. As such, these amendments were merely tokens and did not represent real reform. Upon adoption, no one knew what the impact of the Bill of Rights or the meaning of these amendments would be.[8] The Alien and Sedition Act controversy would test Americans' assumptions about the Bill of Rights.

A little more than twenty years after Americans declared independence and less than ten since they had ratified both the Constitution and Bill of Rights, Congress, with the initial support of the people, enacted a series of laws that limited some of the very rights these documents promised to protect. What were the circumstances that allowed such laws to pass? How did Americans and their political leaders react to the revolutions in France and rebellions elsewhere in Europe, especially Ireland in 1798? Could politically radical immigrants who were fleeing government oppression in their own countries be integrated into American society? Could or should they become citizens? Did they pose the same apparent danger to the established government as they did in their native countries?

Federalists and Democratic-Republicans answered these questions differently. Americans were not only struggling with an influx of immigrants, but they were also grappling with defining the scope and shape of their new nation. In the 1790s, the Constitution was the dominant political issue—how to interpret it, what the powers of the executive were, what the proper balance between the national and state governments was. Americans asked throughout the decade what their republic should look like. They asked what the people's role in political debate ought to be. Should the people only be heard during elections, or should they be free to voice their opinions at any time? Where and how could the people and even opposition politicians properly voice their disagreement with the administration? When did dissent become treason?

These questions figured prominently in political debates leading up to 1798 and the passage of the Alien and Sedition Acts. From 1798 through the Election of 1800, these matters became more pressing as US security and independence seemed particularly at risk from both foreign and domestic sources. Historians have answered these questions in a variety of ways. Significantly, the Alien and Sedition Acts and the controversy they created present issues that are still not fully resolved today.

1 Governing a Republic

"THE UNION: WHO ARE ITS REAL FRIENDS?" asked the title of a 1792 newspaper article by James Madison. In it, Madison asked the readers of the *National Gazette* to consider which political leaders truly represented the people. The Union's real friends were not those who sought to give the government "unlimited discretion, contrary to the will and subsersive [sic] of the authority of the people." Rather, its friends were those who opposed the "spirit of usurpation and monarchy" and advocated for a republican policy.[1] Even posing this question exposed the growing divisions among Americans. In the series of articles of which this was one, Madison explained how he and his friends disagreed with Alexander Hamilton about the meaning of the Constitution and extent of federal government power. These disputes during George Washington's presidency raised issues that would continue to be debated during the Alien and Sedition Acts controversy later in the decade. Amid the controversies over the Neutrality Proclamation, Whiskey Rebellion, the Jay Treaty, and finally Washington's Farewell Address, the nation continued to argue about the proper role of the people in a republic. The political parties of the Federalists and Democratic-Republicans and the public were engaged in a decades-long debate.

The Federalist and Democratic-Republican Parties emerged during the first half of the 1790s as a result of a series of disputes over domestic and foreign policy. At first, the disagreements were largely confined to the cabinet and Congress, but the rivals—Secretary of State Thomas Jefferson and Representative James Madison on one side and Secretary of the Treasury Alexander Hamilton on the other—soon connected these internal governmental clashes with the broader ongoing public debate.

These men, along with George Washington and John Adams, were the dominant political figures of the decade. Washington, Jefferson, and Madison were members of the Virginia gentry and served in various state and national political offices during the Revolution and thereafter. Washington's conduct during the Revolution had earned him the admiration of the nation. By serving as chair of the Philadelphia Convention, he gave the gathering immediate legitimacy and authority. The new government under the Constitution received a similar benefit when Washington agreed to serve as president. With the deep respect and trust of the people, Washington was able to stay above the disagreements and fighting among his cabinet secretaries and between Hamilton and members of Congress during his first term. But even Washington would eventually succumb to partisan political battles during the latter part of his presidency.

Washington's fellow Virginians emerged as the loudest voices of opposition to his policies. Jefferson was governor of Virginia during the Revolution and served in the Continental Congress, where he drafted the Declaration of Independence. After the war, Jefferson represented the United States in France. While in Paris, Jefferson witnessed the heady early days of the French Revolution. Upon his return to the United States in 1790, President Washington appointed him secretary of state, a role in which he increasingly clashed with Hamilton. Jefferson resigned in 1793 and soon emerged with Madison as leaders of the opposition to Washington's administration, and especially to Hamilton. That opposition would eventually become the Democratic-Republican Party.[2] Jefferson's friend and political ally, Madison had also thought long and hard about how best to govern a republic. Plagued by poor health throughout his life, Madison could not serve in the military, but he held a variety of political posts, including in the Confederation Congress and Philadelphia Convention. He cemented his national reputation through his role in the crafting of two seminal founding documents—the Constitution and Bill of Rights.[3]

In preparing for the Philadelphia Convention in particular, Madison thought deeply about the problem of federalism: the distribution of powers and responsibilities, which were sometimes shared, between the state and national governments. Because Madison believed that the structure of government—the complicated distribution of overlapping powers of the state and federal governments and the proper balance of power and checks among and within governments—would best protect the people's rights rather than "parchment barriers," he initially opposed a bill of rights. Partly as a result of Jefferson's arguments from Paris that "Half a loaf is better than no bread" and the pressure from Anti-Federalists, Madison eventually became of proponent of a bill of rights, reasoning that "it is anxiously desired by others."[4] Although Jefferson and Madison worked closely in opposition to Federalist policies, they were not always in complete agreement, as was the case in the debate over a bill of rights. They challenged each other to refine and occasionally moderate their own views as they faced repeated domestic and foreign policy crises.

Unlike Jefferson and Madison, Hamilton was not born into a family whose wealth and social status meant that public service and political leadership were assumed. Instead, Hamilton was born out of wedlock, was orphaned at a young age, and had few prospects when he arrived in colonial America from the British West Indies as a teenager. Yet Hamilton was intelligent and ambitious. He had proven his financial smarts managing a business at home, which won him the support and sponsorship of some of the island's most prominent men. Once in New York, he studied at King's College, now Columbia University, where he quickly caught up with his younger classmates and became involved in the radical patriot movement at the start of the Revolution. During the war, he proved himself to be an able and loyal aide-de-camp to General Washington, to whom his political fortunes would be forever linked. Washington appointed him as the first secretary of the treasury.[5]

These men and the political parties they would help lead later in the decade had different ideas of what the American Republic should be. These differences translated not just into specific policies but also into how each party engaged the people, and how the people engaged the government as well. They had distinct conceptions of the people's role in government. For Hamilton and the Federalists, the people's role was to express trust and support for their leaders. The people should stand with and behind the government to give the government strength and legitimacy. Without the confidence of the people, the government's authority would be weakened. This confidence, they argued, was particularly important for young nations that did not possess long track records of effective governance. On the other hand, Jefferson, Madison, and Democratic-Republicans believed the people should watch the government to ensure that their rights were safe. Government policies, they believed, should be derived from the collective opinions of the people, not the other way around. So, instead of offering what was basically unconditional support, Democratic-Republicans envisioned a more active, participatory citizenry. Madison asserted, "Public Opinion sets bounds to every government and is the real sovereign in every free one." A republican government had to act according to the will of the people. The people should be critics and supporters, not just the supporters and the occasional critics Federalists wished them to be.[6]

While the parties imagined different roles for the people, neither Federalists nor Democratic-Republicans distinguished the policies of a particular administration from the government as a whole. Americans associated opposition with corruption and disloyalty that could flirt with treason. For many, there was no difference between the policies of government and the nation itself. Thus Madison and Jefferson did not simply disagree with Hamilton's policies, but believed that Hamilton's policies would render the Constitution meaningless, turn their republic into a monarchy, and ultimately destroy the Union. Hamilton labeled Jefferson and Madison's opposition not as part of a healthy debate but as a direct threat to the government and thus the nation's very existence. Legitimate opposition could be expressed during elections, but other opposition, especially the kind Democratic-Republicans mounted, was illegitimate and verged on treason, according to Hamilton and the Federalists. These distinct visions of the proper role of citizens influenced how political leaders addressed the public and viewed the proper role of the press.

—

Early on, it became clear that the conflicts between Hamilton and Jefferson would not be contained within the cabinet. Newspapers regularly printed the House of Representatives' debates (the Senate met in secret until 1794). The newspaper-reading public could easily follow the events in the capital. Increasingly through the 1790s, the debates and other news were printed with partisan editorials. The partisan press and political parties grew together. Hamilton and Jefferson saw the value of using newspapers both to attract and retain supporters. Hamilton's vehicle was the *Gazette of the United States*, which was published by John Fenno. At first, Fenno envisioned his enterprise as the official government paper and moved his business when in 1790 the capital moved from New York to Philadelphia, where Hamilton employed him as the Treasury Department's printer. Hamilton even extended him several personal loans when financial failure threatened Fenno's enterprise. As political controversy heated up, Fenno quickly shifted from merely reporting what the government did to defending it from its critics. Jefferson and Madison countered the *Gazette* by helping Philip Freneau, the "Poet of the Revolution" and a friend of Madison's from college, establish his own paper, the *National Gazette*. Because newspapers were rarely profitable on their own, Jefferson gave Freneau the job of translator in the State Department, with assurances that he would have ample time to devote to the newspaper. Madison began to write for the *National Gazette* from its inception; Jefferson, as was his policy, did not write for newspapers but certainly urged others to do so. Essays by Freneau and Madison in late 1791 and early 1792 focused on the themes of consolidation, broad construction of the Constitution, threats to republican government, and risks of the United States becoming a monarchy. It was in one of these essays that Madison posed the question about the Union's friends. The *National Gazette* identified Hamilton, not Washington, as the chief villain. It was during these first newspaper wars that Madison and his allies began to call themselves Democratic-Republicans.[7]

While these particular newspapers eventually failed, they helped create the partisan press. Other unapologetically partisan papers replaced them, including Benjamin Franklin Bache's *Aurora*. In fact, Bache changed the name of his paper in November 1794, after he had been printing for nearly three years, to the *Aurora*, with the promise that his paper would "diffuse light within the sphere of its influence,—dispel the shades of ignorance, and gloom of error and thus tend to strengthen the fair fabric of freedom on its surest foundation, publicity and information."[8] Bache thus positioned his newspaper as stridently partisan and forcefully Democratic-Republican. Newspapers routinely shared and reprinted material from other papers. Pieces from Bache's *Aurora* appeared throughout the country in a network of Democratic-Republican newspapers. The same was true of Federalist papers, although their network would not be as extensive. News of demonstrations and riots in Philadelphia traveled throughout the country, and Philadelphians likewise learned of meetings in Kentucky and elsewhere. The newspaper wars of the early 1790s proved to Federalists and Democratic-Republicans how valuable newspapers could be as a tool to shape and harness public support for their cause. In 1791–92, many newspapers changed from purely business enterprises to vehicles of partisan politics. While some newspapers attempted to remain neutral, increasingly as the decade proceeded and especially after the passage of the Sedition Act, newspaper editors were forced to choose sides.[9]

Newspapers did not just report domestic news; foreign news took a substantial portion of their pages as well. Just as domestic and foreign policy merged on the newspaper pages, so it did in American minds. Domestic policy issues about financing the government, paying the debt accumulated during the Revolutionary War, and conducting government business may have fueled the initial disagreements among political leaders, but foreign policy ultimately defined the differences between parties. The foreign policy questions that produced the most acrimony were about America's relationships with Great Britain and France—one a former enemy and the other a supposed ally. Federalists believed that the United States could not afford to antagonize Great Britain, its biggest trading partner and the nation with the largest navy. Democratic-Republicans argued that the United States should reward its friends, particularly France, and not its enemies. The foreign policy debates would only intensify with the French Revolution and the subsequent European wars.

When the French Revolution began in 1789, it energized many Americans who welcomed the creation of another republic. They saw the French Revolution as an extension of their own and believed that it was their duty to support a sister republic in a world dominated by monarchies. Such support was reflected in public demonstrations. In the early 1790s, celebrations of the French Revolution—Bastille Day, French military victories, French-American Treaties of 1778, and the new French constitutions—dominated the public festivals and commemorations. Americans found an event associated with France or the American-French relationship to celebrate with parades, feasts, and toasts seven months of the year. At the beginning, the majority of Americans embraced the French Revolution. Within a few years, as it became both more radical and brutal, American support faded. First it was the more conservative Federalists who withdrew their support, but by the end of the decade, Democratic-Republicans too grew more uncomfortable with the course the French Revolution.

The decline of American support was marked by several key events. Perhaps the first news that shook Americans was that of the 1792 September Massacre, when 1,500 people, many of them priests, were murdered. Conservative American religious leaders, particularly in New England, interpreted the massacre as an attack on religion. They quickly withdrew any support that they had once given the French revolutionaries and urged their congregants to do the same. Then the news of the king's execution in January 1793—quickly followed by the French declarations of war against Great Britain, the Netherlands, and Spain in February and March of that year—furthered weakened Americans' enthusiasm. The final blow to popular American support was when Americans learned of the Reign of Terror, which lasted from September 1793 to July 1794 and saw 20,000 to 40,000 Frenchmen executed. The Reign of Terror particularly frightened Americans with its brutality and seemingly arbitrary treatment of the government's political enemies. Furthermore, French actions did not seem to threaten stability only in Europe but throughout the world as well, including in the United States. In November 1792, the French National Convention decreed that republican revolution was a universal right and pledged French aid to other nations. Federalists interpreted this decree as just one more piece of evidence of aggressive and destabilizing behavior by the French.[10]

In addition to monitoring the events in France, Americans were also concerned about the revolution in the French colony of Saint Domingue, now Haiti, led by former slave Toussaint L'Ouverture. Haiti was the richest colony of any empire at the time, and France desperately wanted to hold on to it. This revolution, inspired by the French Revolution's language of equality and freedom, was long and violent. It began in 1791, and the Haitians did not declare independence until 1804 with the establishment of a black-led nation. In between, the French abolished slavery in 1794 and then tried and failed to reestablish it in 1802. When Great Britain invaded the island in 1793, many white planters allied with them and against the French. Throughout the course of the Haitian Revolution, an estimated 20,000 refugees, white and black, came to the United States, about half of them during the 1790s. Historians estimate that about 5,000 of them were black. They went to American cities from Philadelphia, Pennsylvania, to Charleston, South Carolina. The refugees shared their stories of violence, atrocities, and near escapes. Often they arrived with little but what they could carry aboard the ships. White Americans expressed sympathy for the refugees as well as fear that their presence could further destabilize America. In particular, slaveholders believed that the enslaved Haitians would spread ideas of rebellion and insurrection among their own slaves. In Virginia, for example, while the state government was providing monetary assistance to the refugees, local governments were pleading with the state for assistance to protect their residents against these outsiders. And it was not just that Southerners were wary of a foreign slave population corrupting their own, but also many Americans did not trust the political allegiances of the white refugees. Supporters of the French Revolution, like Jefferson, believed the white planter refugees who quickly and easily shed their allegiance to republican France for monarchist Britain were as much of a potential danger as the slaves they brought with them. White Haitians never successfully shed their reputation as "monocrats" and aristocrats.

Americans certainly felt sympathy for the refugees and extended aid to them in many forms. Yet many Americans were overwhelmed by the refugees' needs. When private and state philanthropy and patience ran out, refugees and their friends turned to Congress for help. While considering the humanitarian issues, congressmen also debated the constitutional issue of whether the Constitution empowered the federal government to give such aid. In 1793–94, Congress justified limited help as aid to an ally and applied the allocated funds against their debt to France from the American Revolution, skirting the constitutional issue. The federal government provided no aid thereafter. Aid became an exclusively local and state concern.

It was perhaps the presence of these refugees, whose arrivals came in waves in 1791 and again in 1798, that most dampened Southerners' enthusiasm for the French Revolution.[11] Until the Civil War, one only need to mention Saint Domingue to convey what could happen if slavery were debated or the nation ceased to support the institution. When Southerners believed that their institution was under attack, they accused the North of wanting to turn the South into another Saint Domingue or of wanting to try the same experiment with black rule in the South. These statements were warnings to the whole country of the potential dangers of meddling with the institution of slavery. Southerners would stoke such fears during the Alien and Sedition Acts debate, especially with regard to the Alien Friends Act.

—

The prolonged war between England and France, which began in 1793, created deep divisions among Americans. Federalists favored friendlier relations with Great Britain, and Democratic-Republicans were more willing to forgive French misbehavior in order to preserve the relationship forged in revolution.

The partisan differences became more pronounced and the subject of public debate with the arrival of the French minister to America, Edmond Genet, and Washington's proclamation of American neutrality in the European war. In the struggle to win the people's support, pro- and anti-administration leaders sought to win and prove public backing through public meetings, petitions, and newspapers.

Instead of sailing directly to Philadelphia, Genet landed in Charleston, South Carolina, in April 1793 and traveled over land to the temporary capital. Along the way, towns and communities feted Genet and the French Revolution. By the time he arrived in Philadelphia, he thought Americans fully supported his cause. In view of such support, Genet initiated the nondiplomatic part of his mission: to boost French military ambitions by commissioning privateers to attack British ships in the Caribbean and by preparing plans for the French invasion of Spanish Florida and Louisiana.[12] While Genet was immersed in celebrations, banquets, and other plans, Washington's cabinet considered how they should respond to the European war and Genet's escapades, and whether the French treaties of 1778 were still valid. Although Washington eventually requested Genet's recall to silence the minister, he could not so easily resolve the disputes within his cabinet or quiet public debate. His cabinet secretaries all agreed that the American Union would not survive involvement in the European war, and thus the most prudent policy was neutrality. The question became how to explain this decision to the American people. The disagreement that erupted between Jefferson and Hamilton was about executive versus legislative power. Jefferson and Madison argued against the executive issuing a proclamation because they equated the declaration of no war with the power to declare war, which rested with Congress. Hamilton countered that that was not the issue. If laws existed that stated or implied American neutrality, then it was the executive's responsibility to administer those laws. Washington issued the Neutrality Proclamation on April 22, 1793. In it, he declared that the United States would "adopt and pursue a conduct friendly and impartial toward the belligerent Powers."[13] Furthermore, he warned Americans that if they engaged in any activities that violated or compromised American impartiality, they would not receive the protection of the government.

Hamilton quickly realized that the proclamation needed to be explained to the people, and the best way to do that was to use newspapers. Beginning in late June, he launched a series of essays in the *Gazette of the United States*, signed "Pacificus," defending Washington's actions. His essays stressed the executive responsibilities and the energy required in government, especially in foreign affairs, the necessity for the United States to clarify its position regarding the European war, and the obligation to put America's own security above its treaty obligations to France. When no one immediately answered Hamilton, Jefferson urged Madison to "take up your pen, select the most striking heresies, and cut him to pieces in the face of the public." Madison did just that in his "Helvidius" essays, in which he made the case for legislative supremacy over the executive. He countered Hamilton's call for executive energy with dire warnings about the usurpation of power by the executive. The dangerous concentration of power in the president could easily lead to despotism and tyranny. The dispute pitted executive discretionary power against legislative superiority, which would again be at issue during debates about the Alien and Sedition Acts. This essay war shows that both Hamilton and Madison, although they had different conceptions of the proper role of the public, saw the people as an entity worth fighting over.[14] Newspapers like Fenno's and Freneau's proved to be an effective forum for this battle. In a government based on the consent of the people and a political culture that valued and believed in one common good, political leaders with increasingly divergent and incompatible views believed that they had to fight for the people's hearts and minds.

Despite Hamilton's efforts, Federalists believed they were losing that battle. Federalists expected the people to obey the government. The problem was that the people did not understand the proclamation to be law and thus something to be taken seriously and obeyed. In at least one instance, a jury acquitted a seaman of violating the terms of the proclamation because the jury rejected the idea that a proclamation was the same as a law. Federalists remedied the people's confusion by passing a neutrality law in June 1794. In addition, Federalists redoubled their efforts to prove that the people endorsed the policy by organizing meetings that adopted resolutions supporting Washington and his policies. By responding favorably to the resolutions and memorials produced by public meetings, Washington condoned these practices and means by which the people could express their confidence in the government. By publicizing the meetings and their resolutions in newspapers, Federalists could show that the people not only supported the neutrality policy but also trusted the government to do what was right. The meetings and memorials demonstrated that the people stood with Washington. Nevertheless, the meetings did not fully or even truly represent all of the people.[15] Many of the issues debated during the neutrality crisis, especially the scope of executive power, would resurface during the Alien and Sedition Acts controversy. Significantly, the strategies that the parties employed in 1793 would be used again in 1798.

As demonstrated during the debate on the Neutrality Proclamation, Americans were divided about how to legitimately express their disagreements in a republic. Some of those who opposed Washington's policies believed that the only way their political voices could be heard was to form their own groups, independent of the government. They called themselves Democratic Societies or Democratic-Republican Societies or clubs. In part inspired by both the American and French Revolutions, these groups began as political clubs to discuss politics and ended up as an important voice of opposition to both Washington's administration and their own state and local governments. The first society was founded in Philadelphia in 1793 with some valuable advice and encouragement from Genet. At their height, there were forty-two clubs spread among almost every state. In general, these societies recognized the French Revolution as a continuation of the American Revolution, opposed Hamilton's financial policies, considered Washington to have betrayed the Revolution, and most importantly wanted to reinvigorate republican ideals and create a vigilant citizenry that would protect the legacy of the Revolution.[16] As one club asserted, "The eyes of the republican patriot must ever be watchful; and as many characters have crept in among us, who are not with us, their steps should be carefully watched."[17] These societies diagnosed the problems in both the state and national governments as being similar. Their elected representatives had failed to fulfill the promises of the Revolution by enacting policies that seemed to benefit the few over the many. The groups played an important role in challenging the idea of unconditional support for the government, casting doubt upon the Federalist idea that the people and government were one. Instead, they embraced the ideas that government decisions should be the result of free debate among the people, the people should form government policy, and government should be responsive to the people. Significantly, they used newspapers to publicize their activities. Newspapers regularly reprinted resolutions from societies in other states; for example, a club in Pennsylvania could learn about a club's activities in New York, South Carolina, Kentucky, or Massachusetts, and vice versa. There was a remarkable similarity in language and sentiment among many of the societies' public declarations, whether it was asking for the reform of state penal codes, greater support for public education, or the abolition of federal excise taxes. Local and regional issues became national ones. Democratic-Republican Societies helped to nationalize politics through their use of newspapers. This aspect certainly troubled Federalists, but what disturbed them more were the societies' claims that they spoke for the people. For Federalists, only the government could speak for the people. The presence of these other voices in opposition to the government threatened the stability and survival of the nation by weakening people's trust and confidence in their governments.

The Democratic-Republican Societies' demise occurred within the context of the Whiskey Rebellion in western Pennsylvania. Although it was the largest armed uprising between the ratification of the Constitution and the Civil War, the Whiskey Rebellion was at its heart about defining legitimate opposition to government policies. While Pennsylvanians were not the only ones to refuse to pay the federal excise tax on whiskey, their proximity to the capital made them good candidates of which to be made an example. The rebellion reached its height in summer 1794, just as Americans' support for the French Revolution seemed immune to the atrocities in France and the widening European war, and the Democratic-Republican Societies were thriving.[18] Federalists connected these seemingly disparate events. What they saw was an increasingly unstable world that they believed endangered their republic. America was not immune to the chaos in the rest of the world. In fact, the people seemed susceptible to the disorganizing ideas of European radicals.

At first, western Pennsylvanians voiced their opposition to the law in ways Federalists would have approved. They petitioned their representatives in Congress and the state legislature for relief and repeal of the tax. None of these petitions was answered positively. Frustrated that neither the state nor federal governments heard their voices, westerners resorted to long-used tactics of resistance, including nonpayment of taxes, and harassment of tax collectors and their neighbors who paid their taxes or cooperated with authorities in other ways. Their tactics were not new or innovative, but their target was different—the federal government, not the state. The whiskey tax became a tangible symbol of what the rebels believed was wrong with the country. Taxation had been a central issue in the Revolution and continued to be so after. In the early 1790s, tax resisters in western Pennsylvania and the members of Democratic-Republican Societies in eastern cities and rural areas (including western Pennsylvania) voiced similar complaints about both federal and individual state tax and land policies, which they saw as favoring the wealthy and land speculators. The Whiskey Rebellion was not just about an excise tax on distilled spirits, but also about the way the federal government financed the Revolutionary War debt, the national bank, state land policies, and the unresponsiveness of both the Pennsylvania state government and the federal government to the people's concerns. The rebellion did not maintain consistent intensity. Although there had been incidents of resistance from the time of the law's passage, the protests and the government's response reached new heights in 1794 with a violent attack on a tax collector's house.

That summer, Washington decided that something had to be done. Upon the advice of his cabinet, he issued a proclamation on August 7 announcing his intention to call out the militia to suppress the rebellion, giving the rebels a chance to end the rebellion peacefully by taking an oath of submission.[19] In the days before Washington issued the proclamation, Hamilton provided Washington with the justification for taking action against the rebels. In a letter that was subsequently printed in several newspapers, Hamilton detailed the protests against the law and the government's response. He emphasized that Congress repeatedly revised the law and confirmed the general sense of community support for the tax. The escalating protests finally forced the government "to meet evil with proportionable decision." Hamilton effectively asked whether the majority should govern or be governed. He admitted that some forms of protest were legitimate, but he narrowed the definition. For Hamilton, one could ask the legislature for repeal or modification of a law, but one could not legally choose to disobey the law. Once the protesters expanded their complaints beyond the excise law to more general complaints that rendered the government "unpopular and odious," protesters crossed the line from complaint to treason.[20] For Hamilton, petitions, memorials, and election campaigns were legitimate; obstruction of laws—violent or not— were not. He both clarified and narrowed the boundaries of acceptable opposition. The people were to support and to express their confidence in the government through obedience to the laws. Therefore the government could legitimately use force to suppress the rebellion.

The Whiskey Rebellion was the first time the federal government used armed force to suppress domestic unrest. It showed in strong terms that violent protest would not be tolerated and that the federal government was willing and able to muster the resources to stop such resistance. This precedent would be in the back of Democratic-Republicans' minds as they mounted their opposition to Federalists' policies later in the decade. Federalists did nothing to persuade Democratic-Republicans otherwise—the use of force by the government was always an implicit threat.[21] When 13,000 militiamen arrived in western Pennsylvania in late October, they found a rebellion that had largely collapsed. Most of the rebels chose submission, but some chose to disappear to the West.

In his Sixth Annual Message in November 1794, Washington explained his decision to use the militia against the rebels to the nation. He criticized these "enemies of order" for threatening the government, but assured the people that the government's character was strong. He asserted that the western Pennsylvanians were not wholly responsible for their actions, but that they had been victims of the "arts of delusion." Washington blamed "certain self-created societies [that] assumed the tone of condemnation." Everyone knew that Washington meant the Democratic-Republican Societies. By "self-created," Washington, echoing Hamilton's letter, narrowly defined the boundaries of legitimate dissent. Opposition could come from constitutionally sanctioned entities—elections, petitions, memorials, and even public meetings with narrow agendas. Elections were expressions of the common good and united the people and government in pursuit of a common goal. For Washington, self-created societies were vehicles for ambitious men who had only their own and not the people's interests at heart. The Democratic-Republican Societies were dangerous precisely because they envisioned a citizenry that was active at all times and a world with no limits on public deliberation. Washington defined the contest in western Pennsylvania and thus the nation as one, between the friends and the enemies of order. The government sought to maintain order and stability. The Whiskey Rebellion and the Democratic-Republican Societies posed a threat to that order.[22] To Washington, violence as a form of protest was illegitimate, and it seemed that groups that the government did not sanction were not permissible either. He articulated a vision of a passive citizenry with a limited role; between elections the people were to support the government. The societies challenged Washington's conception of the people's role before political parties. For them, criticism of the government if it had betrayed the people's interests was both appropriate and required. Such criticisms could not wait until the next election. These same issues about what constituted legitimate dissent resurfaced during the controversy surrounding the Alien and Sedition Acts.

As was the convention then, both houses prepared responses to Washington's message. The Senate wholeheartedly endorsed Washington's condemnation of the Democratic-Republican Societies, but the House balked. Federalists argued that the president should be supported. Representative Fisher Ames of Massachusetts asserted, "The danger is that a Chief Magistrate, elective as ours is, will temporize, will delay, will put the laws into treaty with offenders, and will even insure a civil war, perhaps the loss of our free Government, by the want of proper energy to quench the first sparks." Ames articulated once again the Federalists' belief that the trust of the people, and in this case trust in the people's representatives, was necessary for an effective government. Governors had to be bold and certain of their actions for the Union to survive; they could not hesitate because they feared the people's reactions. The people's role was to support the government so officials could act with energy for the good of the whole. On the other hand, Democratic-Republicans argued that Congress and the people should be able to act independently of the executive. Madison expressed great certainty that the people would reach the correct judgment. "In a republic," he asserted, "light will prevail over darkness, truth over error." He cautioned against establishing a precedent by which the government condemned legal institutions. Democratic-Republicans put forth a different conception of dissent, one that was free of restrictions, except for legal ones, and was independent of the government. Democratic-Republicans defined legitimate dissent broadly; Federalists adopted a narrow definition.[23] In 1794, Federalists successfully silenced the Democratic-Republican Societies with Washington's forceful speech. When they would again try to silence criticism of the government in 1798, Federalists would enact a sedition law to place legal restrictions on speech. Democratic-Republicans argued both times that the government could not effectively restrict what the people said without dire consequences for individual liberty and their republican government.

In the House, Madison had tried to broker a compromise, but privately, he and Jefferson expressed alarm regarding Washington's words, not just for their effect on the people but also because of how Washington narrowly defined what kind of groups could legitimately participate in political discussions. By condemning certain groups who disagreed with the government, Madison feared Washington would create deeper divisions among the American people. Jefferson characterized the message as "one of the extraordinary acts of boldness of which we have seen so many from the fraction of monocrats." He could hardly believe that Washington "should have permitted himself to be the organ of such an attack on the freedom of discussion, the freedom of writing, printing & publishing." Jefferson drew a parallel to the Society of the Cincinnati, an organization founded by officers of the Continental Army and their heirs to promote the Union and the rights for which they fought, in addition to being a benevolent society to help officers and their families. Washington served as president of the society. For Jefferson, the Society of the Cincinnati was a greater danger to the republic because it was hereditary and secretive, whereas the Democratic-Republican Societies were formed to nourish "the republican principles of our constitution."[24] Hamilton and Washington distinguished between associations and self-created societies. Associations like the Society of the Cincinnati were formed for civic purposes like charity. Moreover, the Cincinnati supported the government and did not challenge it, as the Democratic-Republican Societies did. In contrast for Washington and Hamilton, self-created societies were established to satisfy individuals' ambitions. The danger was that these groups, who claimed to speak for the people, did not have the interest of the whole community at heart and would gain too much influence through deceit and cunning.[25] Washington's speech implicitly endorsed organizations like the Society of the Cincinnati by condemning the Democratic-Republican Societies. How political leaders characterized these extragovernmental organizations reflected how they defined legitimate political dissent. These different understandings of how and how much dissent the government could withstand would come into play in the debates over the Sedition Act of 1798.

—

Complicating Washington's reaction to the Whiskey Rebellion, as well as the rebels' own opinion of the federal government, was a series of ongoing diplomatic crises. In particular, the United States clashed with Great Britain over the treatment of neutral shipping and unresolved issues between the two nations that had been lingering since the American Revolution. Every diplomatic crisis had domestic ramifications. The crisis with England in 1794–95, which resulted in the Jay Treaty, solidified party lines and hardened the conflict between Federalists and Democratic-Republicans. During the debate over the treaty, political leaders sought to win the people's support and to demonstrate that support by using the same tactics as used during the dispute over the Neutrality Proclamation. Federalists did not separate the domestic unrest from the turmoil they saw in the rest of the world. Thus the strife at home was directly related to troubles around the globe. Federalists believed that in order to maintain peace at home, they had to insulate the United States from the discord in Europe. Democratic-Republicans worried that Federalist solutions to these problems compromised American independence and neutrality and invited conflict with other powers, namely France.

The crises in 1794 over relations with Great Britain, Spain, and Native American tribes in the Northwest Territory were interrelated. One could not be resolved without the others. First, the ongoing controversy with Spain over navigation rights to the Mississippi was resolved with the Treaty of San Lorenzo in October 1795. Second, the Indian tribes in the Northwest Territory signed the Treaty of Greenville, in which they ceded much of the Ohio Valley to the United States and established a clear boundary between Indian lands and white settlements. Finally and most importantly, the United States and Great Britain negotiated an easing of tensions with the Jay Treaty, which included British compensation for seized American ships and also their withdrawal from forts in the Northwest Territory. The British departure meant that Indians lost a crucial source of protection against Americans, which made the Treaty of Greenville possible. For Westerners like the Whiskey Rebels, it seemed the government was finally able to provide at least some of the security that they wished for and that the government was being responsive to their concerns. Yet these crises exacerbated the existing divisions throughout the country.

The relationship with the British proved to be most controversial and had significant effects on American political divisions. In late March 1794, Washington learned that the British had seized hundreds of neutral ships. Talk of war with Great Britain increased, and Congress took some initial steps by imposing a one-month embargo, which was largely seen as a precursor to war, and increasing the size of the military. These measures were fraught with political significance because they were debated as the Whiskey Rebellion escalated. With relations with Britain deteriorating and the domestic situation uncertain, Washington appointed Chief Justice John Jay to negotiate a settlement with Great Britain. Jay returned with a treaty in the early summer of 1795. The treaty itself satisfied no one completely, but it did help to alleviate the immediate crisis with Britain and to open the Northwest Territory to white settlement.

Significantly, the treaty precipitated a months-long debate in the cabinet, in the Congress, and among the people, which solidified party lines. There were numerous public meetings organized, newspaper articles written, and petitions signed throughout the summer and fall of 1795 and the early winter of 1796. While political leaders on both sides acknowledged the people's commitment to republicanism and the republic, they believed that the people were susceptible to appeals from monarchists, as Democratic-Republicans called the Federalists, or Jacobins, as Federalists called Democratic-Republicans. Monarchy and Jacobinism represented foreign ideas, and thus neither had a place in America. Both parties believed they had to rescue the people from these evils and save the republic. The Jay Treaty was the proxy for these arguments because it was characterized as either the work of monarchists or as protection against Jacobinism. For Democratic-Republicans, the treaty abandoned neutrality, sacrificed American independence to Britain, and violated the treaties of 1778 with France. For Federalists, the treaty repaired America's relationship with England, its largest trading partner, and preserved neutrality. Whether you thought the treaty betrayed a friend or made America more secure would determine whether you were a Democratic-Republican or Federalist.[26]

Once the Senate ratified the treaty by the constitutional mandated two-thirds majority on a vote of 20 to 10, party leaders shifted their attention to the public and to the contest to win the people's support. Bache printed the full text of the treaty, which had been kept secret by order of the Senate, after receiving a copy from a Democratic-Republican senator. Bache believed that once the people read the full treaty, they would understand that the Federalist government did not have the nation's true interests at heart. Hamilton and his fellow New Yorker Rufus King took up their pens and authored thirty-eight "Camillus" essays defending the treaty and attacking public meetings against it. At one public meeting, at which Hamilton insisted on defending the treaty, the anti-treaty crowd forced Hamilton to retreat, although accounts differ as to whether the crowd "dragged him through the gutter" or drove him away by throwing rocks and perhaps grazing his head. Whatever the actual truth, Hamilton was not seriously injured.[27] As they had done in support of the Neutrality Proclamation in 1793, Federalists organized an effective petition campaign in favor of the treaty, demonstrating the people's support of the government. In opposition, Democratic-Republicans conducted their own newspaper campaign, held their own anti-treaty public meetings, and tried to defeat the treaty in the House of Representatives. In the House, Madison led the Democratic-Republicans in a failed effort to derail the treaty by refusing to appropriate the funds needed for its implementation. They were stymied by Federalists' effective petition campaign and the threat to not ratify the treaties of San Lorenzo and Greenville if Democratic-Republicans refused to fund the Jay Treaty. Madison and others eventually conceded defeat.[28] Federalists successfully demonstrated that they had the people's support.

The controversy over the Jay Treaty deepened the divide among Americans. The political alliances that had formed during the debates about Hamilton's financial policies and neutrality now solidified into more or less permanent political factions. This turn of events bothered most leaders, as they still did not accept political parties as a positive good. Instead, they saw them as a sign of failure. In a political culture that valued consensus, parties represented irreparable conflict and corruption. Democratic-Republicans in opposition justified their party by arguing that the government had been seized by men who did not have the country's interests at heart, and they needed to form a party to combat the threats of aristocracy and monarchy. Their "band of patriots" only existed to right the nation's direction. Once in power, their party would dissolve, as there would no longer be any need for it. Federalists, or "the friends of order," had a similar attitude toward parties. Their purpose was to provide stability and to protect the American Republic from the invasion of Jacobins and other foreign radicals.[29] Clearly, each group was intent on destroying the other. Neither party separated the government from the administration. To oppose the government was to oppose the republic and Union, and to govern was to embody the nation. For Americans in the 1790s, then, there could be no middle ground. This persistent anti-partyism was the backdrop of all political debates during this period. Each party perceived the other as illegitimate and thus to be destroyed. So while the Jay Treaty eased the tensions between the United States and Great Britain, it intensified the conflict among Americans and between the United States and France as well.

France viewed the Jay Treaty as a betrayal of the promises of its own treaties with America made during the Revolutionary War and as a signal of an emerging American-British alliance. Subsequently, France issued a secret decree authorizing the seizure of neutral ships. With relations with France deteriorating, Washington recalled the American minister, James Monroe, from his post. In the last months of his presidency, Washington appointed Charles Cotesworth Pinckney of South Carolina, who although a Federalist was enthusiastic and sympathetic to the French Revolution. One of the wealthiest men in the state, Pinckney had welcomed Genet upon his arrival in Charleston, although later Pinckney would disapprove of Genet's activities. Even though Pinckney was supportive of Washington's policies, he was a moderate rather than a zealous partisan.[30] For Washington, Pinckney was a good compromise because he could both satisfy Federalists at home and be acceptable to the French. Nevertheless, the French refused to receive the new minister and expelled him from the country in January 1797, deepening the crisis in Franco-American relations just before John Adams took office.

—

In September 1796, Washington announced his retirement with the publication of his Farewell Address. Written with Hamilton's help, the address was both a defense of his presidency and an articulation of his vision of the republic. In it, Washington warned of the dangers of factions and parties, but he focused on sectional divisions as being particularly dangerous. In a reference to the Whiskey Rebellion, Democratic-Republican Societies, and the Democratic-Republican Party, he predicted dire consequences if such groups were allowed to fulfill their true purpose, which he saw as subverting the regular processes of government—elections and deliberation. These extra-constitutional groups or self-created societies could "become potent engines by which cunning, ambitious, and unprincipled men will be enabled to subvert the power of the people and to usurp for themselves the reins of governments; destroying afterwards the very engines which have lifted them to unjust dominion." Washington suggested that liberty was best protected by the government—a government "with powers properly distributed and adjusted, its surest guardian."[31] By characterizing the opposition to his government as a dangerous threat to the republic, Washington articulated one justification that would be used for the Alien and Sedition Acts.[32] In his farewell, he counseled the people to have confidence in the government and trust that its institutional arrangements would protect them.

—

During Washington's presidency, Americans grappled with a variety of issues regarding both foreign and domestic policy. Political leaders engaged the public through newspapers and pamphlets. The people expressed their support or disapproval of the government through elections, public meetings, petitions, memorials, and occasional acts of violence. Conflicts centered on different visions of the new nation and the definition of what it meant to be an American. They struggled with not only the substance of issues but also how to conduct politics, especially how to disagree with each other. They did not separate a particular administration with the fundamental institutions of government or the Constitution—these were one and the same. Almost all opposition could thus be seen as a sign of corruption as well as treason by those who controlled government, and as a patriotic effort to save the country from its current rulers by those on the outside of government. These issues of what constituted legitimate dissent and how to go about disagreeing with the government remained unresolved at the end of Washington's presidency and were central to the storm over the Alien and Sedition Acts only a couple of years later. Just as troubling was Federalists' belief that the source of the opposition was not wholly domestic, but that foreigners—particularly the French and Irish—were manipulating and exciting the opposition against Federalist policies.

2 Extreme Revolution, Vexing Immigration

AT THE ANNUAL DINNER of the Hibernian Society for the Relief of Emigrants from Ireland in March 1793, several of the toasts would have alarmed Federalists had they been in attendance. This group of Irish immigrants celebrated the French Revolution and "all who arm in the cause of the *Rights of Man*," a direct reference to Thomas Paine's book defending the French Revolution and advocating the right of revolution. They saluted religious and political freedom and expressed the hope that the "*Universe* be formed into one *Republican Society*, and every honest man enjoy the blessings thereof." This society had originally been founded in 1790 as a charitable organization to serve the growing Irish immigrant population, but within a few years, it had become affiliated with Democratic-Republican Party politics. After their arrivals in the United States, William Duane, John Daly Burk, and other Irish immigrant printers would also join the Hibernian Society. Federalists saw such societies as home to dangerous radical political ideas. The Hibernian Society connected poor immigrants to politically radical immigrants and then to the national Democratic-Republican leadership.[1]

Federalists believed that the influx of European immigrants fleeing war and political turmoil exacerbated American divisions. In the political conflicts of the late 1790s, recent immigrants were more likely to identify with the Democratic-Republican Party than with the Federalists. Even as the Federalist and Democratic-Republican political parties became more a part of the political landscape, Americans continued to express discomfort with the ideas of political parties and institutionalized political conflict. They still identified the government, the Constitution, and the nation as one and the same. The war in Europe, the continued conflict with France, and the increased numbers of European radicals seeking safety in America would lead Federalists to the conclusion that comprehensive defense measures that addressed threats from both without and from within were necessary to protect America from the turmoil in Europe. Federalists saw the instability around them and identified immigrants as one threat to American security and unity. Such analysis of the situation led them to question both the utility and ability of these aliens to become American citizens. Over the course of 1797 and the first half of 1798, the crisis only seemed to worsen.

The Constitution contains few barriers to citizenship and full participation in the American polity, with the notable exceptions that presidents must be native born or to have been citizens when the Constitution was adopted, and that members of the House and Senate must be citizens for at least seven and nine years, respectively. Beside those provisions, the Constitution grants the Congress responsibility for establishing a uniform rule of naturalization and grants to citizens of each state the privileges and immunities of the other states, thus allowing free people to move easily across state borders. The Constitution did tie voting to states by specifying that the qualifications for voting in federal elections were the same as those requirements for state legislatures' lower houses. States thus retained much of the authority over newcomers within their borders. Although the federal government established the qualifications and process for citizenship, the states determined some of the privileges of citizenship, like voting and owning property.[2] The federal government established the requirements for citizenship, and the states determined the rights of citizens. The Constitutional Convention left responsibility over citizenship divided and ambiguous between the states and the new federal government.

Naturalization, and thus citizenship, in the American Republic represented a departure from British concepts of citizenship. With independence, Americans reconceived citizenship to be voluntary and contractual. In effect, people could after a probationary period choose the United States as their country and renounce their citizenship in their native countries. In contrast, Great Britain considered citizens to be subjects of the king, and therefore citizenship was by birth and permanent, meaning, for example, that a person could not renounce his English citizenship in order to become an American. In the United States, an immigrant could become as good a republican as a native-born citizen. Through residency requirements, immigrants could both learn about and prove their dedication to American principles and ideals. Political leaders did not always agree on the ideal length of residence necessary to accomplish this education.[3] As the crisis of the late 1790s intensified, some leaders even voiced doubts about whether immigrants could truly become Americans at all. Although such arguments were usually quickly rejected, the fact that these ideas were even entertained demonstrates the depths of the fear immigrants generated at the time.

The debate about citizenship that was central to the controversy surrounding the 1798 Alien and Sedition Acts fundamentally changed after 1792, when the French and Haitian Revolutions were in full force and partisanship was intensifying in the United States. Before 1792, most would-be Federalists and Democratic-Republicans alike had viewed the United States as a refuge for the "oppressed and persecuted of all Nations and Religions."[4] In addition, most American leaders had welcomed newcomers as a way to address persistent labor shortages. After 1792, with the increase in immigrants fleeing war and oppression in Europe and the development of political parties in the United States, Americans' attitudes toward immigration took a decidedly partisan turn, with Federalists wanting to increase restrictions and Democratic-Republicans desiring a more inclusive definition of citizenship. Each party's own self-interest also played a role in immigration policy, as the new immigrants tended to vote with the Democratic-Republicans and not with the Federalists. Federalists already believed Democratic-Republicans were not loyal Americans but French Jacobins, and therefore immigrants' affiliation with their opponents only confirmed their belief that these immigrants posed a threat to the nation. Increasingly, Federalists defined a true American as one who supported, not opposed, the government. Democratic-Republicans were not immune from projecting their fears onto new immigrants. Each party had its own particular set of fears: Federalists of radical French Jacobins and their British and Irish sympathizers, and Democratic-Republicans of anti-republican aristocratic refugees from France and Haiti. In 1794, these fears manifested themselves in the effort to revise the Naturalization Act of 1790, which had required only two years of residency for free whites to qualify for citizenship.

The debate to revise the naturalization law began in 1794, at a time in which Federalist discomfort with immigrants also exhibited itself in the controversy over seating Albert Gallatin, a Swiss-born Pennsylvania Democratic-Republican, in the US Senate. Federalist senators challenged the length of Gallatin's residency in Pennsylvania, and thus his citizenship, by claiming that he had not met Pennsylvania's own citizenship requirements. Gallatin countered that his active participation in the American Revolution qualified him for citizenship even though he could not offer the specific evidence of his residency that Federalists now required. The Pennsylvania legislature, which elected Gallatin, considered Gallatin a citizen. On a party-line vote, Federalists denied Gallatin his seat. Democratic-Republicans concluded that Federalists were willing to take advantage of the ambiguous citizenship laws and poor record keeping to deny their opponents offices. Consequently, Democratic-Republicans would be suspicious of Federalist motives in future naturalization debates.[5]

Shortly after the Senate denied Gallatin his seat, Pennsylvanians elected him to the US House of Representatives, where he quickly emerged as a Democratic-Republican leader. In Philadelphia, Gallatin built upon his reputation gained while serving in the Pennsylvania state legislature as an expert on public finance and advocate for entrepreneurs and small farmers. He was a credible, knowledgeable critic of Hamilton's management of the Treasury Department. To the chagrin of Federalists, Gallatin even called for the investigation of Hamilton's official conduct. Although he was one of the leaders in quelling the Whiskey Rebellion and restoring order in western Pennsylvania in 1794, Federalists associated him with the unrest in the area. Despite efforts to silence him, Gallatin became a constant and forceful voice of Democratic-Republican opposition in the House. During the Alien and Sedition Acts debates, he often complained that he was the only Democratic-Republican willing to speak out against Federalist proposals. He remained a thorn in the side of many Federalists. Refusing to grant Gallatin a Senate seat did nothing to silence his criticism of Federalists.[6]

In 1794–95, the debate over revising the Naturalization Act was about both parties trying to protect the nation from the different dangers that each party had identified, signaling deeper partisan conflict. A consensus emerged that aliens posed some danger, although each party defined that danger differently, and therefore a longer residence was necessary for these aliens to truly become Americans. The law increased residency requirements from two to five years. Political leaders agreed that citizenship was based on consent, and that people could choose to renounce citizenship in one country to become a citizen in another.[7] But significant differences emerged, which only became more pronounced during the 1798 debate. Some Federalists doubted whether a naturalized American should be able to hold office because, they argued, he did not have the necessary early education in "republican character." Federalists cast aspersions on all adult aliens and naturalized citizens as being not fully capable of holding citizenship with all its obligations and privileges. Democratic-Republicans articulated their fears in proposed amendments requiring aliens to declare their "attachment to the [r]epublican form of government" and to renounce all claims to hereditary titles and nobility. Certainly, Democratic-Republicans were thinking about the aristocratic Haitian refugees living among them. Federalists were, too, when one introduced an amendment requiring immigrants to renounce claims to their slaves. This proposal failed, but only after Southern Democratic-Republicans defended the rights of property and accused the proposer of fanning the flames of slave insurrection at home. After a contentious debate, the final law contained the requirement that aliens repudiate claims to titles of nobility, but it did not prohibit naturalized citizens from holding office or require swearing an oath to a republican government. Significantly, Federalists were also able to insert the condition that naturalization would adhere to the federal standards, prohibiting the use of often more lenient state naturalization procedures.[8] This issue of state versus federal responsibility for naturalization would again arise in 1798, when Federalists succeeded in excluding state participation in the process of naturalization altogether. Over the course of the 1790s, the Federalists' definition of citizenship became increasingly narrow, restrictive, and nativist. To be an American meant to support the government, and for a group of Federalists it also meant to be born in America. In contrast, Democratic-Republicans' concept of what it meant to be an American remained broader, more lenient, and inclusive, with no obligation to support the current government but with a general commitment to republican government and a repudiation of aristocracy and monarchy.

Immigrants posed particular challenges for both Federalists and Demo-cratic-Republicans. Federalists were more wary of immigrants' potential im-pact, which they believed would be mostly negative on America's security, stability, and future. Democratic-Republicans, although concerned about roy-alist immigrants, were more optimistic about aliens being able to integrate successfully into American society.

Throughout the 1790s, with each instance of strife and unrest in Europe and Haiti new groups of immigrants and refugees came to the United States. The influx of immigrants came not just from France and Haiti but also from Great Britain and Ireland. Approximately 80,000 people emigrated from Great Brit-ain and 60,000 from Ireland between 1790 and 1800, many more before 1798 than after. More Irish emigrated in 1798 during the Irish Rebellion, whereas more English came earlier in the decade, during a period of government re-pression there.[9] Approximately 30,000 Frenchmen were also living in the United States in the late 1790s.[10] Many of the French immigrants chose to reside in Philadelphia, which was then the nation's capital. In the mid–1790s, more than ten percent of the city's population was French.[11] Many of them, too, had looked to America as both a place where they could find like-minded people and a safe haven from the chaos of revolution. Many of these immi-grants had left their home countries because of their political views. Federal-ists tended to see every one of them as a potential enemy.

Among the French, Federalists did not distinguish between those who sup-ported or opposed their country's ongoing revolution. As the French govern-ment changed hands numerous times during the decade, it was easier for Federalists to suspect all of them than to try to understand the differing politi-cal views among the émigrés. In fact, Democratic-Republican Gallatin esti-mated that ninety-nine percent of the French living in America were hostile to the French Revolution. Their ultimate wish was to return home, although many of them could not safely do so because the newest regime considered them enemies. Edmond Genet, the French minister to America in 1793, was among those who could not safely return after Washington requested his re-call. Genet avoided the guillotine by staying in New York, marrying a daugh-ter of that state's Democratic-Republican governor, and eventually settling on a farm on Long Island.[12] Nevertheless, Federalists were particularly con-cerned with those French émigrés who had been active participants in the French Revolution. One example was Comte de Volney, who was a scientist and author. His most famous work argued that revolutions happened when existing governments did not follow principles of natural law, equality, and liberty. He and Thomas Jefferson had met in Paris when Jefferson was serving as the American minister to France. In 1796, Volney spent three weeks visiting Jefferson at his home, Monticello.[13] Jefferson believed that Volney in particular was a Federalist target, and he was correct. Federalists found men like Volney dangerous not only because of their political views but also because Americans, especially leaders like Jefferson, were blind to the threat these men posed to America's security.

Volney and others were not completely innocent. As the French government moderated and the American government became more extreme and less welcoming, these Frenchmen became more willing to aid the new French government and less concerned about alienating some of their American hosts. Volney, Georges-Henri Victor Collot, who was one of the few men to have a deportation order drawn up for him under the Alien Friends Act, and others traveled throughout the western United States and into Spanish territory. They speculated in lands, but more importantly they gathered information about both the geography and loyalties of the people living on the western frontier, which they reported to Pierre Adet, Genet's successor as France's minister to the United States. The French government would likely have wanted to use this intelligence to help them in their ambitious plan to reestablish a French empire in North America. Especially since the United States ratified the Jay Treaty, France no longer considered America to be a reliable trading partner or ally.[14]

Although officials in the American government may not have known the full scope of the Frenchmen's missions or plans, Federalists suspected that they were up to no good and posed a danger to America's security. Federalists frequently accused the French of causing the collapse of other nations' governments from within by sending spies and emissaries to create domestic dissention and unrest. The agents would succeed by alienating the people from the government, resulting in revolution. Federalists were certain that the same fate awaited the United States if the French agents and spies were allowed to roam the country freely and woo susceptible Americans with their charms. One newspaper warned of Volney and men like him: "Americans! Beware—at this moment beware of the diplomatic skill of the French republic."[15] Federalists believed that once the American people realized the danger these immigrants posed, it would be too late. These fears even affected American treatment of the French diplomatic corps. President John Adams refused to accept the credentials of the new French consul to America, another one of Jefferson's acquaintances, and even signed a blank warrant ordering the consul's father's deportation if he chose to come to the United States. The man instead chose to delay his planned emigration to America until after the current crisis was safely over. Jefferson believed that Federalist policy was directed against men of science and learning, those whom he most wanted to come to the United States. Federalists did not see these men as scientists but as potential foreign agents charged with undermining American stability.[16]

It was not only the French that Federalists believed would threaten America; they also saw the recent exiles and immigrants from Ireland and Great Britain as a danger. Federalists tended to focus their attention on those immigrants who had been active in radical politics at home and continued to be so once they arrived in the United States. The Irish were engaged in a rebellion against British rule, which the British brutally suppressed over the course of 1798. British actions increased pressure on some in Ireland to leave and raised concerns among some Americans that the British were exporting their rebellious population and related problems to the United States. Of further concern was the fact that the Irish rebels had welcomed a French invasion and engaged in talks with the French about providing them with some military aid. Federalists feared that Irish immigrants hoped the same fate would await the United States and that, when the French invaded America, these Irish immigrants, along with the French aliens, would happily join the invading forces and turn against their American hosts. In fall 1798, the American minister to England, Rufus King, sought explicit promises from the British government that they would not deport Irish prisoners to the United States, as had been widely rumored.[17]

These fears were not without some foundation. Many of the Irish immigrants who had been involved in the rebellion as members of the United Irishmen established similar organizations in America. In Ireland, this group was a secret, revolutionary organization that plotted to overthrow British rule and establish an independent republican Ireland. Inspired by the French and American Revolutions, these Irishmen in America continued to support their collaborators at home, and many became active in American politics, where they connected the current struggles in Ireland to previous ones in America. John Daly Burk, who would be indicted for sedition in America, wrote a history of the Irish Rebellion in which he drew parallels not just with the

American Revolution but also with the recent Whiskey Rebellion.[18] He saw the Irish in 1798 and the American rebels of 1776 and 1794 as being engaged in the same timeless struggle against an oppressive government. The Irish immigrants who joined United Irishmen groups in the United States were more likely to be recent arrivals. The new immigrants, among whom was William Duane, who took over the *Aurora* after Benjamin Franklin Bache's death, tended to identify themselves with the Democratic-Republican Party in America. For them it was an easy transition; even if the groups' methods differed, many of their core principles—such as freedom of thought and equal opportunity—were the same. In the late 1790s, Duane helped establish the United Irish Society to promote the establishment of republican government in Ireland. In addition, he founded a Democratic-Republican militia company in Philadelphia called the "Greens," made up entirely of Irish immigrants.[19]

For Federalists, Duane's militia company was ready-made to aid the French in the event of an invasion. The United Irish Society and United Irishmen posed the same threat to American stability and security as the French. Federalists made that connection for the broader public by often calling Irish immigrants Jacobins. While some would wear the label with pride, others rejected such name-calling. By labeling these recent Irish immigrants as Jacobins, Federalists categorized them as foreign and not wanted in the United States.[20] Older immigrants, who were more likely to identify with the Federalist Party, were wary of the newer immigrants. They blamed the newcomers for causing the unrest in Ireland and for bringing their "disorganizing principles" to their new home. While many of these immigrants had come to the United States believing that they would be able to enjoy the rights and liberties that they had been denied at home, they found an America struggling to define those very rights and liberties itself.

—

News, commentary, and analysis of the French Revolution, Irish Rebellion, and the European War found a place in American newspapers and pamphlets. Americans learned about European events and movements not necessarily from the immigrants themselves but from American newspapers, whose source for European news was British newspapers. Just as Americans had supported and opposed the cause of the French Revolution with public demonstrations, newspapers too expressed their opinions regarding the Revolution and the ideas the revolutionaries espoused on their pages. Printers like Bache saw their papers as a way to express their political views even at the expense of profits and perhaps invite financial ruin. Many editors saw themselves as political players, and they were willing to use their businesses to further their political cause. They aimed to create an engaged citizenry who advocated and defended equality and democracy. Their newspapers and pamphlets contained stories about mostly European men who had sacrificed their lives and freedom for democracy.[21] These stories certainly held relevance to these ideas in America. These pamphlets and articles connected the events in Europe to those in America, which was exactly what Federalists feared.

Bache and others also gave recent political refugees a forum in which they could express their political views and reflect upon the parallels between their recent experience of political oppression and the potential for it in America. Duane, James Thomson Callender, and Thomas Cooper—all of whom would be indicted under the Sedition Act of 1798—were employed by Bache and other like-minded printers shortly after their arrivals in the United States. Based on their experience of political oppression in their native countries, these writers spoke out against the suppression of speech and the press in America. For Federalists, these writers highlighted the dangers that immigrants posed to American security. The foreign influence on newspapers worried Federalists because they came to believe that the American Republic could not withstand the constant assault of criticism that these newspapers hurled at political leaders as well as, Federalists believed, at all Americans. Thus the political debates of the 1790s were not just about particular policies but also about what it meant to be an American citizen. The 1796 presidential election would in part be about just that—the influence of foreigners in American politics.

—

The Election of 1796 was the first presidential contest without George Washington. It was also the first to involve political parties, with John Adams the Federalist candidate and Thomas Jefferson the Democratic-Republican candidate. America's relations with France and Great Britain were major issues in the campaign, and Jefferson and Adams represented a stark contrast with regard to foreign policy. The Jay Treaty with Great Britain and France's hostile reaction were the central issues in many states. The intensity of the presidential contest and how much the people were engaged fluctuated greatly from state to state. Although the Constitution established the number of each state's delegates to the Electoral College, states determined how those delegates were chosen. Selection—which included election by the state legislature, by the people, and a combination of these methods—varied from state to state and election to election. Pennsylvania voters in 1796 chose delegates, and thus the election was particularly hard fought. Federalists' fears about foreign influence in America came directly into play.

On the eve of and directly after the Pennsylvania election, Democratic-Republican newspaper editor Bache printed a series of three letters from Pierre Adet, the French minister to America, to Secretary of State Timothy Pickering, even before Pickering had had the chance to properly translate and officially transmit the letters to either the president or to Congress. The letters detailed France's resentment against Washington's administration. Adet told Americans that the nation's relationship with France depended on the outcome of the election, and reinforced the idea that the election was about choosing war or peace. If Americans elected Adams, surely the result would be war with France. If they wanted peace, they should elect Jefferson. Adet made it clear whom France preferred. In his second letter, called the "cockade proclamation," he called on all Frenchmen in the United States to show their support for their country by wearing the tricolor.[22] The public flaunting of one's connection to France played directly into Federalists' fears that resident aliens would choose their native country over America in the event of an invasion or a war, and that these guests in America would gladly foment discord in their host's country. For Federalists, Adet's letters and Bache's printing of them were further proof of French treachery, of the danger posed by Frenchmen residing in the United States, and, most significantly, of Democratic-Republicans' disloyalty. Once again, Federalists saw evidence that Democratic-Republicans were tools of the French. They also believed that French spies were everywhere, and that the French were determined to interfere in America's domestic affairs. This incident confirmed Federalists' wariness of not just the French but also immigrants in general, who they believed threatened to destabilize America.

Although Jefferson won Pennsylvania, he lost the election to Adams by a handful of votes. Philadelphia Democratic-Republicans thought that Adet's letters had boosted their cause, which allowed them to win the state. Yet Democratic-Republicans outside of Pennsylvania saw drawbacks of such a bold move. James Madison told Jefferson, "Adets Note . . . is working all the evil with which it is pregnant."[23] Adet's letters only gave credence to Federalists' arguments of the danger France and foreigners in general posed. France, by interfering in an American election, did not respect America's independence or sovereignty. Adams won the presidency, and because there was no separate ballot for vice president, the candidate who finished second, Jefferson, became vice president. Adams's slim victory indicated how closely divided Americans were.

Unlike many of his contemporaries, Adams made no secret of his political ambitions; he wanted to be president. He had waited for the opportunity through eight years as vice president, an office he called "the most insignificant office that was ever the invention of man contrived or his imagination conceived."[24] Despite his larger political ambitions, Adams wrote freely about his political philosophy. In *Thoughts on Government* (1776) and *The Defense of the Constitutions* (1787), Adams outlined his beliefs about the best structure of government. *Discourses on Davila*, which he wrote in response to the French Revolution, was his most controversial piece. This 1791 pamphlet picked up on earlier themes about the natural divisions in society and the need for those divisions to be reflected in the structure of government. *Discourses* went further, claiming that places like France and England needed a monarchy and aristocracy for stability. Adams's desire for stability led him to endorse a lifelong presidency and hereditary Upper House for America. He believed that these measures were the only way to properly balance and protect all the interests in society. *Discourses* cemented many Democratic-Republicans' belief that Adams was reflexively anti-French and dangerously pro-aristocracy. Throughout the remainder of his life, Adams would try to explain these views. Jefferson's criticism of *Discourses* would lead to a falling-out between the two men that would not be repaired until after Jefferson retired from the presidency in 1809.

—

When Adams was inaugurated on March 4, 1797, he faced an immediate crisis with France. France had increased its attacks on American shipping in retaliation for the Jay Treaty, which France saw as a violation of its own treaties with America from 1778. Thus began the so-called Quasi-War, a series of naval conflicts lasting from 1796 to 1800. Adams had to address what seemed like an increasingly dangerous situation. Although Adams had extensive political and diplomatic experience, he had no executive experience. He did little to build support within his cabinet, Congress, or the public for his policies, which he viewed as exclusively the purview of the executive. In addition, Adams saw his administration as a continuation of Washington's. Accordingly, he retained Washington's cabinet, with whom he had a difficult and problematic relationship because they were often more loyal to Hamilton or their own faction within the Federalist Party than to him. Adams believed that the current crisis with France could be resolved in the same manner as Washington had resolved a similar crisis with England, when John Jay successfully negotiated a treaty. Instead of appointing one man to negotiate a settlement, Adams wanted a commission of three: James Madison of Virginia, Charles C. Pinckney of South Carolina, and Elbridge Gerry of Massachusetts. Adams believed that these commissioners would provide more geographical than partisan balance. Significantly, Adams first reached out to Jefferson and not his own cabinet. Jefferson rejected Adams's overture; he had become too much of a partisan leader to cooperate with a Federalist administration. In contrast, Adams did not identify himself as a Federalist; instead, he envisioned his role as executive as independent of the partisan politics, a view that would seem increasingly old fashioned. Madison had no interest in serving as a member of the commission, and Adams did not find a warm welcome for his nominations from his cabinet, either. Accordingly, Adams replaced Madison with John Marshall of Virginia, a young, moderate Federalist from a Democratic-Republican state. Adams eventually won some lukewarm support from the cabinet for the mission.

Gerry, the only Democratic-Republican, was not fully trusted by either his party or diplomatic colleagues. Although he had a long record of public service in the Continental Congress, Philadelphia Convention, and the House of Representatives, he had a nervous character and seemed caught between his fears of aristocracy and monarchy on the one hand and excessive popular democracy on the other. Abigail Adams expressed sympathy for her husband's great friend when she wrote, "Poor Gerry always had a wrong kink in his head." Gerry's personality was offset by Marshall's gregarious and relaxed manner and Pinckney's moderation. Marshall, as a result of his service in the Continental Army during the Revolution, was a confirmed nationalist. He emerged as the unofficial leader of the Federalist Party in Virginia when he actively supported Washington's Neutrality Proclamation and the Jay Treaty. Washington had previously appointed Pinckney as minister to France, but France refused to receive him. When Adams nominated him to this mission, Pinckney had been spending his exile in Holland.[25]

In May 1797, Congress met in a special session to address the French crisis, which had only seemed to have worsened since March with the news that the French no longer considered the "free ships, free goods" provision of the

1778 treaty to be in effect. Americans had a long list of grievances against the French, including the seizure of 316 ships in 1795. French treatment of American ships, cargo, and sailors seemed to have deteriorated after that. In one instance, a French raider tortured an American ship captain with thumbscrews in an ultimately failed attempt to force him to identify his cargo as British and thus ripe for the taking. Before the French let the Americans go, they robbed them of most of their provisions.[26] Adams outlined the French violations of American sovereignty, including attacks on American-owned ships and its refusal to receive Pinckney as minister in his May 16 message. In that message, Adams chose to be both conciliatory and combative. While Adams proposed a peace mission to France, he recommended that Congress shore up American defenses, especially the Navy to protect shipping, in the event the mission failed. At the end, almost as an afterthought or a concession to his cabinet, which wanted it, he asked Congress to consider an expansion of the Army.[27] He did not, as members of his cabinet had advocated, recommend an alien law. He passed the responsibility for figuring out how to pay for these defense measures to the House. Whereas most Democratic-Republicans, even Bache, had given Adams at least their conditional support immediately after his inauguration, following this message, most denounced Adams for desiring war with France. France, too, took offense to Adams's message, which just exacerbated tensions and diminished the chances of a successful mission. France was particularly bothered by the passages referring to French mistreatment of other neutral nations and blaming France for fostering "a division between the government and the people of the United States."[28] This section not only blamed France for interfering in American domestic politics, but it also cast a shadow of doubt over Democratic-Republicans' loyalty to the nation.

In addition to approving the diplomatic mission, Congress seriously debated Adams's recommendations to strengthen the nation's defenses. Democratic-Republicans, however, successfully opposed the Federalists' boldest measures, and Congress took only small steps to enlarge the military. They authorized fortifications of harbors, armed and equipped state militias, and appropriated funds to complete some ships under construction and to improve the Navy. In the midst of these debates, the former American minister to France, James Monroe, arrived in Philadelphia. Monroe, whom President Washington had recalled from his post for leaking details of Jay's negotiations with the British to the French government, was eager to defend his actions as minister. Many Federalists feared that Monroe would undermine the authority of the government and new mission to France. Democratic-Republicans and their friends, some of whom were French, celebrated Monroe's return, much to the mortification of Federalists who questioned Democratic-Republican leaders' judgment in associating with spies.[29] So fraught were both political and personal relationships that Jefferson commented, "Men who have been intimate all their lives cross the street to avoid meeting, and turn their heads another way, lest they should be obliged to touch their hats."[30] Neither Federalists nor Democratic-Republicans believed the other party could be trusted to govern the nation without subverting and violating the true meaning of the Constitution.

—

The debate about what it meant to be an American was revisited during the special session of Congress in May 1797 and again during the debates about the Alien and Sedition Acts the next year. After the 1794–95 naturalization debate, Federalists continued to narrow their definition of an American. By the late 1790s, Federalists had fully renounced the idea of America as an asylum from European oppression to argue that native-born Americans possessed a deeper understanding of American character and values than any alien could have, no matter how long he had lived in the United States. Although the special session of 1797 was mostly devoted to shoring up the nation's defense, it also included efforts to protect against domestic unrest by creating new obstacles to citizenship.

In a debate about taxing certificates of naturalization and thus making citizenship too expensive for many immigrants, Ultra Federalists, a radically conservative faction within the party, expressed their anti-immigrant views. Harrison Gray Otis of Massachusetts, who would champion the Alien and Sedition Acts during the next session, defended the proposed $20 tax on certificates of naturalization by arguing that the tax would effectively end the immigration of "the mass of vicious and disorganizing characters that cannot live peaceably at home," and he urged the House to protect the United States against "hordes of wild Irishmen . . . [who] come here with a view to disturb our tranquility, after having succeeded to the overthrow of their own Governments." In what became infamously known as his "Wild Irish" speech, Otis fully articulated Federalists' worst fears—that the United States would become a place where other countries would send their most disruptive individuals. In turn, these immigrants would directly threaten America's own security and stability.[31] Noah Webster echoed those sentiments when in July he expressed his dismay about the quality of immigrants. For every good and industrious immigrant, he wrote "we receive three or four discontented, factious men . . . the convicts, fugitives of justice, hirelings of France, and disaffected offscourings of other nations."[32] Webster, Otis, and other Federalists wanted to prevent these men both from becoming citizens and from coming to America at all. Although they failed to do so at this congressional session, they would be more successful a year later.

—

Meanwhile, Gerry, Marshall, and Pinckney arrived in Paris in October 1797. Once there, they were confronted with an uncertain situation. The Directory, a group of five men, had controlled the French government since the fall of 1795. They would be displaced by a coup led by Napoleon Bonaparte in November 1799. Leading the negotiations for France was Charles-Maurice de Talleyrand-Périgord. Talleyrand was born into an old noble family. A deformed foot, either the result of a birth defect or an accident when he was an infant or toddler, prevented Talleyrand from embarking on an expected military career, so his parents forced him to transfer his rights as the eldest son to his brother and enter the Catholic Church. Talleyrand found that his real talents and desires did not fit with the Church but with politics. With the advent of the French Revolution, Talleyrand was determined to always be on the winning side. Nevertheless, in 1792, he entered a period of exile for four years. After being expelled from England under their Alien Act of 1793, when France declared war on Great Britain, he went to the United States for two years. In America, he devoted most of his time to making money. Although he much appreciated Alexander Hamilton's political savvy, he was shocked that Hamilton would have to resign from office for personal financial reasons. For Talleyrand, government service was a source of riches, not a drain on them, and he always found ways to make his offices pay handsomely. Upon being appointed foreign minister in 1797, he wrote, "I'll hold the job. I have to make an immense fortune out of it, a really immense fortune." Talleyrand enjoyed remarkable political longevity and served in a variety of French governments—the Directory, Napoleon's Consulate, and the July Monarchy—for more than thirty years.[33]

When the American envoys arrived in Paris, Talleyrand met them with obstruction. His position with the Directory was precarious, and his authority was limited. In addition, he believed, based on his experiences in the United States, that the majority of the American people were sympathetic to France.

Jefferson had been advising French diplomats in America that delay would be the best course because Jefferson and many others believed that France's war with England would soon be over. Peace could resolve the conflicts between the United States and France better than negotiations. Both Jefferson and Talleyrand misread the situation, and Talleyrand's usual political sense failed him in the negotiations with the Americans. Talleyrand's agents refused to meet with the Americans until certain conditions were met, namely, to apologize for Adams's May message, promise to assume French debts owed to Americans, and extend loans or bribes to the Directory and Talleyrand for their private use.

What Talleyrand conceived as a tactic of delay and a potential source of more income became the incident that pushed the nations toward war. The American envoys took great offense at Talleyrand's demands and refused to negotiate on these terms. In his dispatches to Secretary of State Timothy Pickering, Marshall identified the French agents only as X, Y, and Z, thus the incident became known as the XYZ Affair. Marshall and Pinckney stayed in Paris until April 1798, when they left in disgust and defeat. Gerry followed a few months later.

As Congress awaited news of the mission, it tried to carry on with regular business, but the tensions over foreign policy seemed to encroach on every issue. The House occupied itself with the impeachment of Senator William Blount of Tennessee, which for Democratic-Republicans was about fair treatment of Britain and France. Senator Blount was involved in a plot to aid the British in capturing the Spanish territory of West Florida by encouraging Indians in the area to challenge Spanish rule. Although the Senate had expelled Blount during the May 1797 special session for violating the public trust and his duties as a senator, the House insisted on proceeding with the impeachment. Eventually, the Senate dismissed the impeachment, ruling that because Blount was no longer a senator, he could not be impeached. The Blount Affair proved once again the deep distrust both sides had for each other. For Federalists, Blount was one more example of Democratic-Republicans' disloyalty. This time, the disloyalty was even more dangerous because the conspirator was a member of Congress. On the other hand, Democratic-Republicans charged the British with interfering in America's affairs, as the British minister had been implicated in Blount's plot. If the French were abused for interfering in American politics, Democratic-Republicans wanted the British to receive at least the same treatment. Feder-

"Cinques Têtes, or the Paris Monster," 1797. A five-headed monster symbolized the French Directory, whose representatives demanded a bribe from the American envoys (Elbridge Gerry, John Marshall, and Charles C. Pinckney). Marshall retorted, "Cease bawling, Monster! We will not give you six pence!" A mixed-race group, including newly freed Haitians, enjoyed a "civic feast" behind the monster. In the background, a woman with a tattered French flag presided over the guillotine, representing the horrors of the Terror. *Source:* Huntington Library, San Marino, CA

alists' improper affinity for the British was confirmed for Democratic-Republicans when Adams did not request the British minister's recall.

Federalists' concerns about radical ideas or dissenting voices were not new in 1798, but the world around them was changing. They believed that the people's proper role was to trust their leaders to pursue the common good. Confidence would give the government the needed energy to provide security, stability, and liberty. Aliens, whether they were from France, Britain, or Ireland, were a potential wedge that could separate the government and the people. Aliens thus symbolized insecurity, instability, and a loss of American independence. While Federalists almost always admitted that there were some good and industrious immigrants, they harbored suspicions about most of the newcomers. To this end, Federalists tried to place barriers to citizenship, including taxing naturalization certificates. On the other hand, Democratic-Republicans did not believe that all aliens posed such a risk, and opposed most of the Federalists harshest measures. They wished for a closer and more constant connection between the people and their governments, especially the national government. Democratic-Republicans understood that the people should play a larger, active role in the political debate. The people's role was not to trust the government but to be ever watchful and jealous of their rights.

The military preparations undertaken during the special session went a long way toward securing America against invasion, but Federalists believed they had not fully addressed the threats from both aliens and American citizens to America's security and independence. By the late spring and early summer of 1798, the majority of Federalists agreed that new naturalization, alien, and sedition laws were absolutely necessary. During the spring and summer of 1798, they would pass four laws addressing these issues that became known as the Alien and Sedition Acts. These laws ignited a debate about the meaning of citizenship, the First Amendment, and the proper role of the people in a republic.

3 Partisan Solutions

ON MARCH 19, 1798, President John Adams officially declared the French mission a failure. Adams announced that he perceived "no ground of expectation that the objects of their [the American envoys'] mission can be accomplished on terms compatible with the safety, the honor, or the essential interests of the nation." He placed the blame firmly upon the French. Then he urged Congress "to adopt with promptitude, decision, and unanimity" measures for defense, both on land and at sea, and to provide the necessary revenue to pay for these additional protections. Adams did not include the envoys' dispatches—their account of the XYZ Affair—with his message, which only added to people's fears and suspicions.[1] Democratic-Republicans assumed that the administration was covering something up. James Madison concluded, "The President's message is only a further development to the public, of the violent passions, & heretical politics, which have been long privately known to govern him."[2] Vice President Thomas Jefferson described the message to his most trusted political friends as "almost insane."[3] To prove Adams and Federalists overreacted and to quiet the calls for war, congressional Democratic-Republicans called for Adams to give the dispatches to Congress, and for Congress to publish them. These Democratic-Republicans did have

Federalist allies who thought publication would bring the nation closer to the war they wished to fight. In the aftermath of the XYZ Affair and the publication of the dispatches, Federalists gained and Democratic-Republicans lost support. Consequently, upon the dispatches' publication, Federalists dramatically increased the pace of legislation. From April through July 1798, Federalists proceeded with the self-assurance that all their actions had one purpose only—to shore up the defenses of the nation. Whether bills addressed the military establishment, relations with France, resident aliens, or domestic dissent, Federalists explained that all were necessary to protect the nation against the immediate French threat.

This program of defense spurred a contentious debate in Congress about the proper role of the people in a republic and whether the government could prescribe that role. Federalists, particularly through the Sedition Act, attempted to define by law the role of the people in the republic, namely, to support the government regardless of their opinions about its current policies. If citizens were dissatisfied with the government, they could effect change through elections or by petitions asking for an alteration or repeal of a law or policy. Democratic-Republicans, in contrast, envisioned a more active citizenry who were always alert to threats to their rights and abuses of power. Dissent, therefore, should not be limited to elections or petitions. Instead, the people's responsibility was to be vigilant and protective of their rights. Democratic-Republicans saw Federalist policies and especially the Alien and Sedition Acts as oppressive and a fundamental change to the character of the republic. These competing visions were ever present as Federalists and Democratic-Republicans considered what to do about the current crisis.

—

In the congressional debate on the Alien and Sedition Acts, Federalists stoked the public's fears about invasion from abroad and, more importantly, how domestic divisions made the United States susceptible to foreign invasion. Federalists' strongest argument was that America's independence was in peril and needed to be protected from the imminent danger posed by the French and their sympathizers—both citizens and aliens—in the United States. Federalists repeatedly connected France to the domestic divisions that they saw as destabilizing the nation. France, they asserted, took advantage of lax and multiple immigration policies and American freedoms, especially those of speech and the press, to infiltrate the nation's politics. The result, Federalists feared, would be to separate the people from their government. Congressman Samuel Sewall of Massachusetts asserted, "It was our weakness, and the division which appeared in our councils, that had invited these attacks. He trusted they should now unite and repel them."[4] The attacks to which he referred were not just from France but also from Democratic-Republicans and others within the United States. Benjamin Franklin Bache's publication of a letter from the French foreign minister in the *Aurora* in June 1798 was for many Federalists confirmation of the existence of a criminal connection with France. South Carolina's Robert Goodloe Harper explained that it had "long been manifest to him that France had her secret agents in this country and that every means had been made use of to excite resistance to the measures of our Government, and to raise a spirit of faction in the country favorable to the views of France." The printing of the letter "was only one of the ramifications of this scheme." Connecticut's John Allen proclaimed as false and dangerous any newspaper article asserting that peace with France was possible and discounting the real risks to America's survival. Allen claimed these "facts" were unfounded; the *Aurora* did profound damage to American unity and would eventually destroy the bonds between man and man as well as the bonds of union. Allen proclaimed, "God deliver us from such liberty, the liberty of vomiting on the public floods of falsehood and hatred of everything sacred, human and divine!" Federalists' policy was driven by their belief that France and the domestic opposition to their policies posed grave danger to the Union.

It was important that the people played their given role as well. Just as Federalists had done during the debates over the Neutrality Proclamation and the Jay Treaty earlier in the decade, they organized public meetings that sent messages of approval directly to the president, and campaigns to send petitions and memorials to Congress. If such addresses, petitions, and memorials were the sole measure of the public's support, then the people overwhelming supported the Federalist program. Adams received about three hundred such messages of support, which shared the language of the petitions and memorials sent to Congress. They pledged their support for all government measures "deemed necessary to defend and maintain its [America's] Honor, Dignity, and Independence." Adams responded to each and every one, just as he did the night he addressed the mob of young men who marched on Bache's house in May 1798. Newspapers reprinted the addresses and Adams's responses, and one printer even collected them in a book. The memorials came from all sixteen states and the territories of Mississippi and the Northwest. Some had thousands of signatures, but a few hundred was more common. Most came from the more Democratic-Republican Middle and Southern states, where the Federalist minority had a great interest in creating the idea of a people united behind their government. Adams could then express his gratitude to the people for their confidence. In response to an address from the Northwest Territory, for example, Adams wrote that never before "have Evidences of the Unanimity of the People, been so decided as on the present Question with France." The Federalist *Gazette of the United States* commented that these addresses were "proof of a remarkable conformity in sentiment and feelings, throughout all of the United States."[5]

In Congress, it was a similar story. From late March through July, as recorded in the *Journal*, the House received seventy-two petitions in support of Adams, and only twenty-six calling for restraint. All but two of these anti-Adams petitions were presented in April and May. Only pro-administration memorials were recorded in the Senate *Journal*. In all, pro-administration memorials outnumbered those opposed by more than four to one. Nonetheless, these numbers are likely a distortion of public opinion, as Federalists challenged and attempted to reject anti-Adams memorials on the grounds that they contained inappropriate language. For example, on May 15, Virginia's Josiah Parker presented the resolutions of Captain Bernard Magnien's militia company protesting the administration's policies. Specifically, they accused the president and "men in high authority" of attempting "to widen the breach between the United States and the French Republic," and they could not approve of efforts that strove "to involve us all in the calamities of a war with the most powerful Republic on earth." They feared that such a war would drive the United States into an alliance with Great Britain, which the resolutions characterized as "the most foul and corrupt Government upon earth." Following the usual procedures, Parker moved to refer the resolutions to a committee, but Federalists objected because the petition was "expressed in language the most indecent and unwarrantable; and if, the House wished to preserve the right of an expression of public sentiment, they ought to guard against the abuse of it." Not all speech deserved to be protected. The House eventually voted to refer the petition by a bare majority only after Democratic-Republican Albert Gallatin of Pennsylvania pointed out the House's inconsistent treatment of petitions. Petitions supporting the president were easily referred; those that did not were subjected to scrutiny and debate.

These actions may have discouraged other Democratic-Republicans from presenting their own anti-Adams petitions. For Federalists, the petitions proved the people's support for their policies.

—

With the nation seemingly behind them, Federalists pushed ahead with the project of shoring up America's defenses, begun during the special session in spring of 1797. Fearing invasion from France and disintegration from within, Federalists sought to make Americans safe as best they knew how. They established the Department of the Navy and authorized the construction of additional frigates and other vessels. In addition, they drastically increased the size of the Army in order to defend against a French invasion. Late in the session, Congress abrogated the Treaties of 1778 and suspended all trade with France and its colonies.[6] These measures, Federalists believed, clarified the American relationship with France short of a formal declaration of war. They represented a compromise between those Federalists who wanted a war and those who preferred to wait. These divisions within the Federalist party bubbled up several times, but as the session wore on from spring into summer and the prospects for peace or accommodation faded with the heat, it was clear that the pro-war Federalists had won the upper hand within their party. For the most part, a small group of Ultra Federalists dominated the floor debates and their colleagues. John Allen of Connecticut, Robert Goodloe Harper of South Carolina, and Harrison Gray Otis of Massachusetts led the House Federalists in fighting the perceived threats to the government, Constitution, and Union.

Allen, Harper, and Otis took control of the debate relatively early in the 5th Congress, pushing for the harshest measures. Harper assumed the chairmanship of the Ways and Means Committee, the most important and prestigious committee in the House. A Massachusetts colleague described Otis as "ardent and ambitious," a reputation he certainly lived up to over the course of his political career. Of the three, Otis was probably the most socially prominent. He came from a well-connected Boston family and graduated first in his class from Harvard. Allen was the most physically intimidating, standing six feet five inches tall and weighing 230 pounds. He cultivated an appearance that was calculated to "inspire dread rather than affection." Unlike Allen and Otis, Harper had flirted with the Democratic-Republican Party. In fact, he had been a pro-France Democratic-Republican when he first arrived in Philadelphia in February 1795, but he quickly converted to Federalism, spearheading

Federalist efforts in South Carolina in favor of the Jay Treaty and during the Election of 1796. The other two arrived in Philadelphia in 1797. Although all three had relatively short House careers, their impact on the 5th Congress cannot be overestimated.[7]

Gallatin and New York's Edward Livingston led the Democratic-Republican opposition, although Livingston abandoned Gallatin for a few months in the middle of the session. Livingston had arrived in the House in 1794 ready to challenge the emerging Federalist Party. He partnered with James Madison to oppose funding of the Jay Treaty. During the Quasi-War with France, he voted against every war measure, including the Alien and Sedition Acts. Livingston was brilliant and spoke eloquently. One biographer describes him as a "temperamental radical who lived 'like a nabob' and talked 'like a Jacobin.'" His eloquence was on full display over the course of the 1798 session. In contrast, Gallatin rarely resorted to Livingston's histrionics and was the more reliable and levelheaded of the two. He did not leave Philadelphia and stayed at his post in the House. He often complained he was the lone voice against Federalist proposals.[8]

—

Federalists believed that strengthening the nation's military defenses was doing only half the job. Led by Allen, Harper, and Otis in the House, Federalists moved to protect America's independence from threats at home. Federalists in the House and Senate worked in parallel on the project. They passed the Naturalization Law first. The alien laws came next, and finally the Sedition Act. In a period when the standing committee system was not well established, the House followed the regular procedure of referring similar issues to the same select or special committee. Most of the military establishment bills and all the alien and sedition bills and resolutions went to the House Select Committee to Consider Means for the Protection and Defense of the Country. By referring all these matters to the same committee, the House leadership indicated that they considered all these measures, including the Alien and Sedition Acts, to be related to and necessary for defense. This committee of seven had only two Democratic-Republican members, one of whom—Livingston—was absent for a good portion of the session. Allen, Harper, and Otis were not among the five Federalists on the committee, but they exerted their influence in other ways.[9]

The House debate on naturalization reflected conflicting visions of what the American citizenry should look like, with Federalists favoring more re-

Robert Goodloe Harper (1765–1825) represented South Carolina and was a Federalist leader in the House of Representatives. He was a forceful advocate and defender of the Alien and Sedition Acts. *Source:* Library of Congress, Washington, DC

strictions and Democratic-Republicans supporting a more inclusive ideal of citizenship. Federalists, like Harper and Otis, envisioned America as a country with a homogeneous citizenry free from the radical democratic ideas of Europe. The people should be distinctly American, unconnected from Europe. Thus Harper proposed that naturalization should be eliminated altogether. For him, strangers "could not have the same views and attachments with native citizens." Nothing but birth should determine citizenship. Federalists and Democratic-Republicans alike rejected these extreme proposals as being unconstitutional, but Federalists insisted that the waiting period to become a citizen be long enough and the process arduous enough that they could effectively slow the process to prevent aliens from ever becoming citizens.

The new naturalization law did indeed make it more difficult to become a citizen. While the 1795 law required only five years of residence before applying for citizenship, the 1798 law increased the residency requirement to fourteen years, which the House settled on as the time an alien needed to form a proper connection to the United States and to loosen the connection to his native country. Federalists believed that if they made the waiting period long enough, they could effectively prevent aliens from becoming citizens, especially the current cohort of particularly dangerous ones, without running afoul of the Constitution. Democratic-Republicans saw no need to erect such barriers.

It was not enough simply to delay citizenship, because many Federalists also believed the government should have the authority to keep tabs on aliens. The new naturalization law required all white aliens to register with the federal district court, the collectors of ports, or an officer authorized by the president within six months if already residing within the United States or forty-eight hours if newly arrived. An alien who did not register would be subject to fines. The clerks of the courts were required to send monthly reports to the secretary of state. Before 1798, immigrants had the choice of applying to either state or federal courts for citizenship. After 1798, only federal courts could grant naturalization certificates. Federalists did not want Democratic-Republican–controlled state court systems to subvert the more stringent conditions of the new law. Thus the law did two new things. First, it created a national registry of aliens, which would make it a lot easier to monitor aliens under both alien acts, and, second, it excluded state courts and officers from processing citizenship applications. Federalists managed to make a responsibility that was once shared by both the federal and state governments into an exclusively federal concern. They effectively narrowed the definition of what it meant to be an American. With a long residency requirement, Federalists effectively prevented new immigrants from becoming citizens, but for them that did not mitigate the present dangers because aliens could still wreak havoc even without citizenship.

With new obstacles to citizenship in place, Federalists turned their attention to resident aliens, who they believed posed a threat that had to be neutralized. Otis believed that stricter measures were called for, as he did not want aliens to have "an opportunity of executing any of their seditious and malignant purposes . . . to seize these persons, wherever they could be found carrying on their vile purposes." He proclaimed that without such a law, "everything else which had been done in the way of defence would amount to nothing." Of the two alien laws, the Alien Enemies Act was less controversial and the only one of the four laws to pass with Democratic-Republican support. The law created a process for expelling alien enemies after a formal declaration of war. It also gave both federal and state judicial officers the power to enforce the law. As Gallatin explained, if any bill respecting aliens was necessary, it was this one, which created a process for the president to deport alien enemies in times of war. Federalists could not argue with Gallatin this time. Unlike almost every other piece of legislation passed by the 5th Congress, the Alien Enemies Act was more a Democratic-Republican measure than a Federalist one. It provided for the orderly deportation of aliens from countries formally at war with the United States. In contrast to the Alien Friends and Sedition Acts, it was drafted without an expiration date.

The Alien Friends Act was a different matter altogether. The original proposal for an alien friends law was made in the Senate in late April, but both chambers toyed with the idea of a law to protect the nation from dangerous aliens. The question was never whether Congress would pass such a law, but rather what provisions it would contain. The Senate's alien bill, which would have restricted aliens' movements to those areas specified in government-issued visas, would have made it uncomfortable for resident aliens to live in the United States. These aliens would have been in constant fear of inadvertently violating the terms of their permits under the surveillance of not just government officials but also their neighbors. The fervently Democratic-Republican *Aurora* called the bill a "statutory monster."[10] House Federalists were not comfortable with the draconian Senate bill; they amended it to moderate the Senate's more punitive tendencies. For example, they struck out the provision that would have imprisoned and subjected to hard labor aliens who returned to the United States after being banished for life. Instead, the House left the length of the sentences to the president's discretion. Interestingly, the House, upon Otis's suggestion, inserted a section assuring aliens, even if they were deported, that their property would be safe. Aliens would be able to take their property with them, and any property left behind would be subject to their control as if they had remained in the United States. This last amendment was not entirely a concession to aliens. Otis wanted to discourage immigrant merchants from withdrawing their money from the Bank of the United States, an important source of credit and loans for Americans and the federal government, simply out of fear it would be confiscated. Finally, the law was not permanent; it would expire on June 25, 1800. The new law granted great discretion to the president to determine which aliens were dangerous and should be deported and which could remain in the United States. It denied aliens access to the judicial system and the protections guaranteed by the Constitution, leaving their fate in the hands of the president and his advisors.

Gallatin led the Democratic-Republicans' opposition to the bill. He challenged the law on the grounds that the powers the bill claimed over aliens belonged to the state governments and not to the federal government. His argument had three components. First, he reasoned that the Constitution did not delegate or grant powers to the federal government over aliens and thus, by virtue of the Tenth Amendment, which declares that powers not granted to the federal government are reserved to the states, the bill was unconstitutional. In addition, Gallatin also cited the slave-trade clause that prohibited Congress from stopping "the Migration or Importation of such Persons as any of the States now existing shall think proper to admit" before 1808, but allowed Congress to impose a tax not exceeding $10 on such persons before that date. Democratic-Republicans interpreted this clause to pertain to both enslaved people and immigrants because "migration" implied voluntary movement. The federal government therefore could not place any restrictions on immigration, and the bill was unconstitutional. Southern Democratic-Republicans raised the possibility that if the president could deport seditious aliens, then certainly the same law could be used to deport enslaved people and thus become an instrument of emancipation. Because enslaved people were not and never could have been citizens, they remained aliens regardless of their place of birth. Southerners introduced the specter of the revolution in St. Domingue, present-day Haiti. They implied that any hint of the possibility of large-scale emancipation invited the prospect of rebellion, violence, and revolution.

Lastly, Gallatin raised the issue of rights. The Constitution guarantees the rights of habeas corpus, jury trials in criminal cases, and due process. Gallatin argued that because the Constitution uses "persons" and not "citizens," these rights applied to aliens as well as citizens. The House bill would have denied these basic civil rights to suspicious aliens. He argued, "so far as relates to personal liberty, the Constitution and common law include aliens as well as citizens; and if Congress have the power to take it from one, they may also take it from the other." Later in the debate, Gallatin asked, "What security . . . can citizens have, when they see a bill like the present passed into law?" If Federalists could be so cavalier with the core rights of aliens as well as with the Constitution itself, certainly they could just as easily curtail the rights of citizens. Jefferson would use these arguments in his draft of the Kentucky Resolutions, written in October 1798.

Federalists were surprised by the use of the slave-trade clause to prove the bill was unconstitutional. They switched between insisting that the clause applied only to slaves and claiming that, if the clause applied to both free and enslaved, then by granting Congress the power to tax enslaved people, it implied Congress had the power to regulate immigration even before 1808. South Carolinian Harper rejected Gallatin's interpretation as absurd. He simply could not take seriously Democratic-Republicans' constitutional objections. He reasoned that if Gallatin was correct, then after 1808 all his "fine-spun arguments . . . will then fall to the ground." And the federal government would possess much more expansive power—to admit foreigners or not—for which Federalists now contended. According to Harper, the only power Federalists claimed for the government was the power to remove such aliens who "are obnoxious to the peace and happiness of the United States." Speaker of the House Jonathan Dayton, as a member of the Philadelphia Convention representing New Jersey, assured his colleagues that the clause, which had been written by the South Carolina delegation, had nothing to do with voluntary immigrants but everything to do with the slave trade. These arguments were the least coherent of Federalists' defense of the bill. Their opponents would continue to use the slave-trade clause as part of their attacks on the laws throughout the public debate that followed their passage.

More persuasive were Federalists' arguments that the Constitution's common defense and general welfare clauses justified the passage of the Alien Friends Act. Furthermore, Federalists insisted that state and federal governments shared power over immigrants. States had the power to admit anyone they wanted to, but the federal government had the right to expel those people once they posed a danger to the safety of the United States. Otis explained that aliens came to the United States under state laws, and if and when they became dangerous, they could have been expelled under federal law. He stated, "it appeared to him an absurd supposition, that Congress has not the power to restrain and to banish persons who may have been sent into this country for the very purpose of spreading sedition and dividing the people, whose intrigues and malpractices threaten the welfare and the very existence of the Government." Federalists reasoned that if the states had the power to deport, then dangerous men would have to be expelled from each and every state before the nation could be safe. Such an arrangement only invited danger and chaos; it did nothing to enhance the safety of the whole nation. As Otis declared, "If we find men in this country endeavoring to spread sedition and discord . . . whose hands are reeking with blood, and whose hearts rankle with hatred towards us—have we not the power to shake off these firebrands?" The Federalist strategy was to take the focus off the law's constitutionality and instead emphasize its necessity. Speeches highlighted the danger posed by recent immigrants. Certainly, if Congress did nothing about these dangerous aliens, America would surely devolve into revolution and chaos.

As the bill passed to its third reading, one step before final passage, Livingston returned to Philadelphia and the House after a nearly two-month absence. Upon his return, Livingston gave an incisive refutation of Federalist arguments. Whereas Gallatin had been detailed and precise in challenging the specifics of Federalist legislation, Livingston delivered a much more sweeping and impassioned attack on his target. He declared that the bill violated the separation of powers. By transferring judicial powers to the president, Federalists would create a despot and "an image of the most fearful tyranny." At least despots legislated openly, but Livingston asserted that the bill made it a crime to criticize the president and thus "a careless word, perhaps misrepresented, or never spoken, may be sufficient evidence; a look may destroy, an idle gesture may insure punishment." Because accused aliens were not to be formally indicted, given a jury trial, allowed to examine the witnesses against them, or have counsel, Livingston railed that "all is darkness, silence, mystery, and suspicion." He raised the alarm that although he had seen measures that he believed violated the spirit of the Constitution, he had "never before been witness to so open, so wanton, and undisguised an attack." The America created by the law would have been one where even intimacies shared by friends could have invited suspicion. One's home did not even offer full security from scrutiny.

Furthermore, Livingston predicted and expected that the people and states would not submit to laws that patently violated the Constitution. In fact, he asserted, "whenever our laws manifestly infringe the Constitution under which they were made, the people ought not to hesitate which they should obey." Livingston called on the people to ignore the law. The disaffection the law would have created among the people exactly what Federalists feared: "tumults, violations, and a recurrence to first revolutionary principles." For the Federalists listening, Livingston's pronouncements seemed even more dangerous than the aliens themselves or what appeared in the newspapers.

Federalists, alarmed by Livingston's calls for resistance to the law, proclaimed his arguments as evidence of the necessity for the law. Otis called Livingston's speech "evidence of the contagion of the French mania." For him, Livingston highlighted the danger at hand. As Otis proclaimed, "When a mind like that of the gentleman is so easily infected, no better evidence need be required of the necessity of purifying the country from the sources of pollution." Harper countered that attempts made to stir up discontent and produce resistance to a law were what was dangerous. These concerns dovetailed with Federalists' fears of sedition in general and explain why House Federalists had initially put issues pertaining to alien friends and sedition into the same bill. Federalists saw the domestic security problem as having two sides, with trouble coming from both aliens and citizens. They hoped that the Alien Friends Act would take care of one side, and a sedition law would take care of the other.

With the alien threat addressed, Federalists could turn their focus exclusively to the threat citizens posed. The Senate acted first on a bill written by James Lloyd of Maryland. Other than a three-year stint in the Senate from December 1797 to December 1800, Lloyd did not hold any other political office. He served in the state militia during both the Revolutionary War and the War of 1812. Otherwise, he seems to have contented himself with the practice of law and the management of his estate.[11] Nevertheless, he enthusiastically did his duty as senator by proposing a draconian sedition bill. Lloyd's bill declared the people of France enemies and proclaimed that giving aid to them was treason, for which the penalty was death. In addition, any person who failed to give information regarding the above activities or engaged in seditious conspiracies or combinations would be subject to fine and imprisonment. Finally, any effort to defame or weaken the government, laws, president, or courts by writing, speaking, or printing anything that could have produced the belief that the government was acting against the Constitution, liberties, and happiness of the people. And such activity would be punishable by fines and jail time.[12] This last provision became the heart of the law.

Lloyd's bill was immediately attacked in the Democratic-Republican press and questioned by Federalists in private. The *Aurora* wanted to know whether Lloyd was exempt from the oath to support the Constitution, to which every federal officer swore and asked, "*Whether there is more safety and liberty to be enjoyed at Constantinople or Philadelphia?*"[13] Hamilton warned that the provisions of the sedition bill were "highly exceptionable & such as more than any thing else may endanger civil War" in a letter to Secretary of Treasury Oliver Wolcott. Hamilton continued, "Let us not establish a tyranny. . . . If we make

no false step we shall be essentially united; but if we push things to an extreme we shall then give to faction body & solidarity."[14] Hamilton wanted to
avoid creating deeper divisions.

In the wake of such criticism, the Senate softened their final bill, which
passed, ironically, on July 4 by a party vote. Senate leaders most likely planned
such a vote not only because of the date's significance, but also perhaps to take
advantage of distracted members. Senator Stevens T. Mason of Virginia described the scene to Jefferson, who had already left the capital for his home in
Virginia. He complained that "the drums Trumpets and other Martial music
which surrounded us, drown'd the voices of those who spoke on the Question. the military parade so attracted the attention of the majority that much
the greater part of them stood with their bodies out of the windows." It was
futile to try to delay action, especially when the bill's supporters included
men like Alexander Martin of North Carolina, whom Mason identified as a
friend. In a forty-five-minute speech, Martin declared his intention to vote
for the unconstitutional bill because he believed it was a lesser evil to violate
the Constitution than to let printers abuse the government. Virginia's other
senator, Henry Tazewell, remarked that passage was "an unauspicious event
to have happened on the 4th. of July."[15] The Senate's bill omitted references to
France, the death penalty, and an expansive understanding of treason beyond
that contained in the Constitution, and instead focused on sedition. It crimi-
nalized combinations or conspiracies that abused the government, and any
writings or speeches against Congress.[16] Still, the bill "excited some clamour
in the City," which led Tazewell to conclude correctly that the bill would not
pass the House as it was, but he had no doubt that a sedition law would be
enacted and "executed with unrelenting fury."[17]

The House, led by Harper, did indeed rewrite the Senate bill, and it was
the House bill that largely became law. It kept the Senate provisions against
conspiracies but substantially changed the sections regarding seditious libel.
The House bill protected not just Congress but also the federal government
and the president. There was no explicit mention of the vice president, who
at the time was the Democratic-Republican Jefferson. The House more precisely defined the crime of sedition to be the speaking, writing, or publication
of "false, scandalous, and malicious" words. The author's intent would have
to be taken into account, and that intent had to be malicious. In addition, the
statement had to be false; speaking or writing the truth was not a crime. The
House, after considering limiting the law to one or two years, finally accepted

Harper's proposal to allow the law to expire on March 3, 1801, which would turn out to be the last day of Adams's presidency.

The House made two significant additions to the bill that modified the common law, which was "judge-made" as opposed to statute law. Common law was a product of court cases, judicial opinions, and jurists' writings about the law. English common law, from which common law in America developed, defined seditious libel as words spoken or written that tended to defame or criticize government or officials. Juries could only decide whether the person had spoken or written the words; judges decided if the content was seditious. Juries could only decide questions of fact, not law. Defendants could not use truth as a defense. In fact, many believed that the greater the truth, the greater the libel. Whether a publication or speech was libel was determined by the amount of damage it could do to the people's confidence in the existing government, not by the truth of the statement. The assumption was that governments could not survive without the good will of the people. In the US House, both Federalists and Democratic-Republicans moved to alter English practice. First, on moderate Federalist James Bayard's motion, the House allowed defendants to use truth as a defense. This amendment was accepted without either debate or a vote. It was likely that members had the case of John Peter Zenger in mind when they adopted this provision. Zenger's 1735 seditious libel case centered on the role of truth. Zenger's lawyer successfully argued before a colonial New York court that the truth of the writing mattered, and that truth could be used as a defense against such charges. While the case did not prove to be a strong legal precedent, it was a political precedent. Between 1735 and the 1790s, several editions of the account of the trial had been printed.[18] Members of the House were most likely familiar with the case and the power of the arguments in favor of using truth as a defense. But Gallatin dismissed truth as no real protection against abuses of the law. Because political writing was opinion and not fact, it would be impossible to prove the truth of an opinion. Gallatin proved correct, as presiding judges in the subsequent sedition trials set such a high bar for evidence that the truth was almost impossible to prove.

The second addition allowed juries to decide questions of both fact and law and triggered a short debate. Democratic-Republican William C. C. Claiborne of Tennessee proposed this amendment because he reasoned that in England it had been the practice for juries to decide only the fact of the publication—whether the defendant wrote, printed, or spoke the libel—and for judges to interpret the law by deciding whether the statement constituted sedition. Harper objected by arguing that it was already well established in America that juries decided questions of both fact and law. Claiborne argued that he just wanted the law to be clear because he believed the doctrine of libels was unsettled. On this issue, state practice clearly differed, as Federalists from Delaware and Connecticut both labeled the practice of giving juries this power "strange" and "most hostile to our system of jurisprudence." Bayard did not trust the unlettered men of the jury to decide questions of law. Congressmen assumed that the practices of their individual state would prevail. With this amendment, the federal law would supersede state customs. The Sedition Act, which Adams signed on July 14, severely limited freedom of speech by criminalizing criticisms of the government and its officers, but allowed the accused to use truth as a defense and juries to decide questions of both fact and law.

During the debate on the law, House members first articulated the arguments that would be refined and expanded in later debates in pamphlets, newspapers, public meetings, and state legislatures. The arguments of Federalists and Democratic-Republicans evolved over the course of the nearly weeklong debate. As they had with the Naturalization and Alien Friends Laws, Federalists again tried to focus on proving the necessity of a sedition law. Allen opened the House debate on the Senate bill by declaring, "If ever there was a nation which required a law of this kind, it is this." Notably, Gallatin had said practically the same of the Alien Enemies Act. Federalists were more than willing to expose the dangers that were all around them. Democratic-Republicans challenged Federalists' conception of the danger and attacked the specifics of the bill, especially the bill's constitutionality, which forced Federalists to explain how such a law could meet constitutional muster. Through the course of the debate, the meaning of the First Amendment—which prohibits Congress from enacting laws "respecting an establishment of religion, or prohibiting the free exercise thereof; or abridging the freedom of speech, or of the press; or the right of the people peaceably to assemble, and to petition the Government for a redress of grievances"—was discussed. Federalists understood the First Amendment's prohibitions regarding the press to mean that Congress could not impose any restrictions prior to publication, like requiring licenses for printers. Once words were printed, the Constitution did not disallow Congress from holding authors and publishers responsible.

Democratic-Republicans had a different understanding of the First

Amendment. They took the prohibitions on restriction for religion, speech, the press, assembly, and petition to be absolute, and thus no restrictions before or after publication were permitted under the First Amendment. In the Democratic-Republicans' speeches on the House floor, they began to articulate an expansive definition of freedom of speech and the press.[19] Both parties, through their discussions of the law's constitutionality and necessity, expounded upon their conflicting theories of the proper role of the people in a republic. Democratic-Republicans expressed their trust in the people's ability to judge their political leaders for themselves; Federalists wished to dictate how and when the people could voice their opinions.

Allen took on the task of proving the necessity for a sedition law—a law that, as Gallatin pointed out, the federal government had not found necessary in its first nine years of existence. Allen proclaimed that dangerous combinations existed, whose purpose was to overturn the government by printing "the most shameless falsehoods" and were "hostile to free Government and genuine liberty." Specifically, he presented several articles from the *Aurora* and New York's *Time-Piece* whose purpose, Allen claimed, was to convince the people that peace with France was possible and that the Federalist government, by rejecting French overtures, was leading the country into a destructive war. Allen claimed these "facts" were unfounded; the *Aurora* did profound damage to American unity and would eventually destroy the bonds between man and man as well as the bonds of union. It was not only the French and Jacobins that Allen feared but also the Irish. Allen quoted from an unidentified paper (but likely the *Aurora*) that had issued warnings to Irish immigrants about the Alien Friends Act and discouraged them from volunteering for the Army. Allen believed that the paper's purpose was to mislead the Irish and "inflame their passions against our Government and against our country." Such writings would turn honest Irishmen into America's enemies. The newspapers were clearly a primary source of danger, and their actions confirmed that a sedition law was necessary.

Allen and other Federalists did not believe that the First Amendment meant that there should be absolutely no restraints upon speech, only that the government could not impose limits before publication. Allen asked if liberty of the press included being able to call the president "a person without patriotism, without philosophy and a mock monarch." Furthermore, did it mean the freedom to call someone a murderer, thief, or atheist? For Federalists, the "freedom of the press and opinion was never understood to give the right of publishing falsehoods and slanders, nor of exciting sedition, insurrection, and slaughter, with impunity." As Allen explained, "A man was always answerable for the malicious publication of falsehood; and what more does this bill require?" Harper dismissed the pleas for protection of the press, for after all "the true meaning of it is no more than that a man shall be at liberty to print what he pleases, provided he does not offend against the laws, and not that no law shall be passed to regulate this liberty of the press." He contended that it was perfectly constitutional to prohibit men from doing what was harmful to society. Liberty of the press should not be possessed by those whose ultimate desire was to abuse and destabilize the government. Otis, in one of the final speeches in the debate, summed up the Federalists view by defining freedom of the press as "nothing more than the liberty of writing, publishing, and speaking one's thoughts, under the condition of being answerable to the injured party, whether it be the Government or an individual, for false, malicious, and seditious expressions." Freedom of the press was "merely an exemption from all previous restraints." The government could stop no one from writing, speaking, or printing anything, but the writer, speaker, or printer was responsible for his own words and could be prosecuted for them.

Over the course of the debate, Federalists more clearly defined the threat they believed newspapers posed. It was the mediating influence that newspapers had between the people and their representatives in government. In particular, Federalists identified a grand conspiracy between Democratic-Republican newspapers and Democratic-Republicans in Congress. Allen understood that the *Aurora* contained "the opinions of certain great men, and certain gentlemen of this House." It was this connection between the party leaders and newspapers that Federalists identified as most threatening. Allen directed his accusations toward the *Aurora*, but he could have been talking about any number of papers: "This is the work of a party; this paper is devoted to party; it is assiduously disseminated through the country by party; to that party is all the credit due; to that party it owes its existence . . . it has flourished by their smiles; it would perish at their frowns." Federalists believed that Democratic-Republican Party leaders controlled the newspapers, and this relationship posed the greatest menace.

While Federalists denied that they did not respect the people or the people's ability to judge government policies and candidates for office, or to understand the issues on their own, not everyone was the people. The people were those who followed the laws; those who opposed the laws were "insurgents and rebels." The people were citizens and voters who during elections exercised the choice to remove obnoxious representatives. Federalists asserted that the people "by the irresistible force of their opinions" forced the government to act. Thus, "when the people wills, the Government is convinced and obeys." In 1798, Federalists saw the relationship between the people and their representatives as subject only to periodic elections as a signal of people's acceptance or rejection of the current elected officials. The constant agitation advocated by the newspapers and Democratic-Republican representatives, especially because it involved resistance to and perhaps outright defiance of the law, struck them as destructive to the confidence and trust the people should have in the government and could potentially destabilize the Union.

In many ways, the newspapers were an ancillary danger. The real threat to the Union came directly from Democratic-Republican members of the House. Allen revealed this concern when he accused his colleagues of spreading lies about the government through their circular letters—public accounts of the business conducted by Congress—which were widely published in the newspapers. Allen was prepared to blame the outbreak of a civil war on these letters, whose object "must be to inflame his constituents against the Government, though at the expense of truth." Harper even conceded that he would have tolerated unfettered freedom of the press, but for members "pronouncing invective against the Government, and calling upon the people to rise against the law . . . this speech may have a very different effect from the filthy streams of certain newspapers; it may gain credit with the community, and produce consequences which all former abuse has failed to do." Federalists had identified these circular letters as dangerous long before the debate on the sedition bill. They had threatened individual members with reprimand and even indictment, without the desired results.

In one instance a few months before this debate, Harper gave notice that sometime before the end of the session he would submit a resolution reprimanding Democratic-Republican Congressman William Findlay of Pennsylvania "for the most vile and unfounded slanders against sundry members of this House." He pointed to a letter recently published in the newspapers that Harper characterized as containing "all that malice and falsehood could suggest for the purpose of defaming the members of this House, and of the Government, and of destroying their reputation." Even the Federalist Speaker of the House believed that Harper in this instance had gone further "than order and decorum would justify." Harper never did introduce a resolution of formal reprimand before Findlay left near the end of the session. Harper seems to have never collected enough evidence of wrongdoing. Individual members were able to frustrate their Federalist colleagues in this respect, but they were not able to stop the Federalists' broader attacks on speech and the press. For Federalists, the fact that the seditious spirit existed among their colleagues, in supposedly respectable quarters, could not be ignored.

Democratic-Republicans immediately challenged Federalists' views on the role of the people in a republic. Virginia's John Nicholas connected the dots for the Federalists. He reasoned that because Federalists, by the rules of the House, could not restrict what members said, the new law would effectively silence them, because members would be prevented from publishing their speeches and sentiments in circular letters or other newspaper pieces. Their constituents would thus be unable to learn about the government. He accused Federalists of creating a domestic tyranny. Democratic-Republicans expressed full confidence in the people to be competent judges of not just their own interests but also whether Congress had overstepped its powers. Placing restrictions on the press would create the suspicion that the government had something to hide. "It was striking at the root of free republican Government, to restrict the use of speaking and writing." Gallatin perhaps had the most reasoned response. By playing on the value Federalists placed on elections, he argued that depriving the people of the means of obtaining information effectively nullified the right of election.

Democratic-Republicans defined freedom of the press in much broader terms than the Federalists. Because the press was the primary source of information for the people, any suppression of newspapers would hinder people's ability to learn about government at best, and at worst create suspicions about government itself. Democratic-Republicans claimed that a sedition law would have created what Federalists wished to prevent, whether that would be the riots and defiance of the law that Livingston predicted or widespread doubts "that there is something in our measures which ought to be kept from the light," as Nicholas suggested. While the law may not have placed any prior restraint on the press, Democratic-Republicans argued that it would have indeed produced such an effect because no man would print a newspaper unless he agreed to say nothing about the impropriety of the government. For Democratic-Republicans, it did not matter whether restraint or suppression came before or after the act of printing, writing, or speaking; the result was the same—the people would be deprived of full information. They understood the First Amendment to mean that "Congress could not pass any law to punish any real or supposed abuse of the press."

Every chance they had, Democratic-Republicans tried to prove the proposed sedition law was unconstitutional because it violated the First and Tenth Amendments. Yet they also challenged the Federalists to prove that such a law was necessary. Democratic-Republicans saw the law for what it was: a party measure. If times were so dangerous, then everyone should be protected and not just Federalist politicians and press. Gallatin rarely seemed to lose his cool or speak with the vehemence that his colleagues spoke with, except on this issue. He reproached Federalists for abusing their power and assailed them for using the law to "delude and deceive" the people by giving them access only to partial information. He declared that "this bill must be considered only as a weapon used by a party now in power, in order to perpetuate their authority and preserve their present places." What they did not admit was that this party measure was a genuine outgrowth of Federalists' belief that the Union, republic, and Constitution were truly under threat and that the only way to combat this menace was to destroy its source—the disloyal Democratic-Republican Party.

After such vigorous and effective attacks on the bill, House Federalists regrouped. It was after these accusations of creating a tyranny that Harper introduced his resolutions and the bill was modified in important ways. On July 10, the House had its final extensive day of debate on the sedition bill, which focused more than any other day on the argument that the bill violated the Constitution because it usurped powers reserved to the states and effectively transferred authority from the states to the federal government. Otis introduced this argument by making the case for both the law's necessity and constitutionality by pointing to state laws and state court cases of seditious libel. Federalists also introduced the law of self-preservation to justify the law. They argued that all free governments had the right to defend themselves against what endangered their existence. Without the means to defend itself, Otis argued, the federal government's independence would be compromised, and it would be rendered dependent upon the states for its protection—a proposition that Otis labeled absurd. Otis again defined freedom of the press as being free from previous constraint, but he maintained it was clearly understood in state and common law that licentiousness and sedition could and should have been punished. Otis believed that juries would be able to make the distinction between truth and falsehood as well as determine whether the accused acted with malice.

Livingston, Nicholas, Gallatin, and others all rose to defend the exclusive power of the states over sedition. Gallatin raised the alarm that although the federal law may not have been materially different from some of the state laws, it did introduce a significant change in jurisdiction by transferring these cases out of state courts and from local juries chosen by the mostly elected sheriffs to federal courts and juries selected by federal marshals. It was the difference between an elective official choosing the jury and an official who was appointed by the president, whose protection was the chief object of the law and served at his pleasure. These members never questioned the states' authority to pass their own sedition laws, just the federal government's power to do so. The First Amendment applied only to the federal government and not to the states. This issue of state sedition laws versus federal ones is connected to the issue of whether a federal common law of crimes existed, as they both had to do with the power of the state governments relative to the federal government.

—

As the minority party, Democratic-Republicans could do little to stop the Federalist majority in their quest to make the nation safe through shoring up its defenses—both external and internal—of the nation. Federalist leaders, by coordinating public meetings, petitions, and addresses to both the president and Congress, created a sense of unity and support for their measures. They believed that they had the full support and confidence of the people to enact what they believed was necessary. This belief may have given Ultra Federalists like Allen, Harper, and Otis the upper hand over their more moderate colleagues. Near the end of the session, Livingston issued a warning against judging the people's confidence by the addresses alone. Federalists should have heeded it.

The Alien and Sedition Acts were an expression of the Federalists' fears about the future of the republic. In order to secure that future, Federalists believed they had to put restrictions upon those living in the United States, citizens and noncitizens alike. Through the Naturalization Act, they hoped to create a homogeneous citizenry uncorrupted by outsiders. The Alien Friends Act would protect American citizens from being corrupted by others. Finally, with the Sedition Act, Federalists tried to establish strict parameters of public debate. If the people wished to express their discontent, they could do so in elections or through petitioning. The laws narrowed the definition of certain rights and who had access to those rights' protections. They were an attempt to define the role of the people in a republic.

4 Self-Inflicted Wounds

BEFORE HIS DEATH in fall 1798, Benjamin Franklin Bache characterized the Federalists' persecution of him as coming "in almost every shape."[1]
As Bache claimed, Federalist harassment came in many forms, both legal and
extralegal. Physical violence, both threatened and real, was committed by
mobs, and judicial and elected officials sought to silence Bache and his paper
through the law. Federalists pursued Bache and others whom they identified as dangerous to the republic with the full power of government and the
law. The crime of sedition is by its nature political because it involves opinion, and thus the trials were political as well. Most of these trials occurred
at the same time as the presidential campaign, which pitted Federalist John
Adams against Democratic-Republican Thomas Jefferson. Federal judges and
Supreme Court justices were partners with the executive branch in their efforts to silence those whom they considered dangerous to the nation. The
judges and justices identified with the Federalist Party and had all been appointed by Federalist presidents, either George Washington or John Adams.
These federal judges were subject to the same fears, concerns, and political
context as Federalists who were elected to office. In part, they saw their role

as supporting the government, not undermining it.[2] Federalist judges and prosecutors used the courts to combat the threats they believed endangered the republic. Indicted Democratic-Republicans responded by using the trials to demonstrate how dangerous Federalists were to the people's basic rights. Participants, judges, lawyers, and defendants saw the trials as opportunities to advance political arguments through these legal proceedings.

Between 1797 and 1801, there were seventeen indictments for seditious speech by the federal government: fourteen under the Sedition Act and three under common law, which had been initiated before the sedition law was passed. Twelve of the people indicted for sedition were printers or somehow connected to that business. The majority of the trials occurred in the spring of 1800 during the presidential election. Adams's administration specifically targeted the major Democratic-Republican newspapers and successfully brought indictments against four of the five of them. They indicted the editors of the Philadelphia *Aurora*, Boston *Independent Chronicle*, New York *Argus*, and Richmond *Examiner*. Only Baltimore's *American* escaped the Federalists' net. Often the accused would hear the charges against him, only to have a trial delayed until the next term. Democratic-Republicans who were indicted in the fall of 1799 were brought to trial in 1800 during the height of the presidential campaign. This timing was likely by design, as Federalists wanted to closely associate the seditious writers with the Democratic-Republican Party and thus discredit their opponents. In the meantime, the accused were released on bail and often continued publishing exactly the kind of material that got them indicted in the first place. Only two newspapers— the *Time-Piece* and the *Mount Pleasant Register*, both in New York—folded because of indictments for sedition, one under common law and the other under the Sedition Act of 1798. One editor, Charles Holt, suspended operations only once he was convicted and in prison. Two editors, Bache and Thomas Greenleaf, died before their cases could come to trial. In both instances, their widows continued their husbands' work. Bache's widow remarried, and her new husband, William Duane, quickly became the object of Federalist suspicion. Ann Greenleaf, who continued publishing the *Argus*, was herself indicted for sedition—the only woman to have been so. All but one of the trials took place in a Northern or Middle state. James Thomson Callender's trial in Richmond, Virginia, was the exception. Interestingly, the strictest enforcement and the loudest calls for arrests were in communities and states with vulnerable Federalist majorities and increasingly bold Democratic-Republican minorities.[3]

Sedition cases were initiated in a number of ways, but Secretary of State Timothy Pickering, who was both the chief strategist and the chief enforcer of the Sedition and Alien Friends Acts, approved all of them. Federalist newspaper editors often called for rival Democratic-Republican editors' arrests. One Federalist New York newspaper declared that Democratic-Republican editors should be "ferreted out of their lurking places and condemned."[4] Sometimes individuals would send offending newspapers or pamphlets to Pickering or the local district attorney. And sometimes Pickering or even President John Adams sent the seditious material directly to local prosecutors, suggesting that they look into the matter. Prosecutions were carefully chosen for maximum effect. Pickering, with Adams's approval, targeted the most influential Democratic-Republican editors and writers whose pieces were widely reprinted and distributed throughout the country. But even the most vehement of Federalists urged caution in how the law was implemented. Fisher Ames, who initiated two cases in his native Dedham, Massachusetts, cautioned Pickering that the "powers of the law must be used moderately, but with spirit and decision, otherwise great risk of disorders will be incurred."[5] Unfortunately for the Federalists, Ames's warning about the potential ill effects of the Alien and Sedition Acts proved more true than false. Federalists often created political martyrs who found ways to continue to challenge Federalist policy, even from jail.

Initially, Federalists attempted to use common law to silence their critics. They brought charges against William Durrell of the *Mount Pleasant Register*, Bache, and John Daly Burk of the *Time-Piece*. In addition, they tried and failed to indict Virginia Congressman Samuel J. Cabell for the contents of one of his circular letters. After the enactment of the Sedition Act, Federalist prosecutors first prosecuted Congressman Matthew Lyon and then the notorious Democratic-Republican writers Thomas Cooper and Callender. Federalists seemed particularly interested in silencing the *Aurora*, which was one of if not the most influential Democratic-Republican newspapers in the country. They charged Bache with sedition, and then on several occasions tried and failed to silence his successor, William Duane. Unlike Lyon, Cooper, and Callender, Duane had a successful newspaper. He did not need a trial to give him a forum. That was precisely what made him so dangerous to Federalists.

—

Because editors Cooper, Callender, and Duane were immigrants, Adams and Pickering considered using both the Alien Friends and Sedition Laws against them. In fact, Cooper and Callender became citizens in order to avoid possible deportation. Yet despite Cooper and Callender's concerns, no one was actually deported under the law, and Pickering and Adams only considered expelling a handful of men. Both Pickering and Adams expressed dissatisfaction with the law's provisions. Perhaps it was its ambiguous yet expansive grant of power, which made some Federalists, particularly Adams, cautious about using it. Perhaps it was that they did not have any experience with deportation, as they had had with seditious libel. Most states had sedition laws, and common-law prosecutions for sedition had been regular, if rare, occurrences since colonial times.[6] Another possibility is that they decided it was safer to let the suspected aliens remain in the United States than to send them back to their native country, where the knowledge they had gained about Americans' weaknesses could be used against the United States. It is most likely that a combination of these factors explains why no one was deported under the Alien Friends Act.

As secretary of state, Pickering, who was a leader of the Ultra Federalists, threw himself into the task of enforcing the Alien and Sedition Acts. He was not one to shy away from using his cabinet position to challenge Adams's leadership and push his own agenda. After the Jay Treaty controversy in 1795 and 1796, Pickering came to believe that Democratic-Republicans would destroy the Union, and he pressed for repressive measures then and thereafter. The Alien and Sedition Acts gave him the opportunity to act on his most punitive inclinations.

Pickering was born in Salem, Massachusetts, but spent a good part of his adult life in Pennsylvania working in the national government. During the Revolutionary War, he served in the Continental Army in various capacities. He achieved one of his greatest triumphs as the special representative to the Seneca Indians early in George Washington's administration, for which he was rewarded with a series of offices—postmaster general, secretary of war, and finally secretary of state. This last office he received only after six other men turned down Washington's offer. Washington's reluctance to appoint Pickering secretary of state speaks to Pickering's lack of diplomatic skill in both his professional and personal relationships. His biographer describes Pickering as extremely self-righteous, with little empathy for those who disagreed with him. Pickering was neither temperamentally nor intellectually suited for the job. After Adams dismissed him in May 1800, Pickering returned to Massachusetts, where he represented the state in the US Senate from 1803 to 1811 and then in the House of Representatives until his defeat in the 1816 Election. During that period, he advocated New England's secession from the Union on at least two occasions and was a fierce opponent of Democratic-Republican policy. It is not surprising that Democratic-Republican editors and aliens dreaded what enforcement of the Alien and Sedition Acts would look like in Pickering's hands.[7]

Some aliens did help the administration by voluntarily leaving the country. French immigrants believed they were particularly vulnerable, especially after the XYZ dispatches were printed. In June, the first group of Frenchmen left the country aboard the *Benjamin Franklin*. Several more ships followed.[8] For dangerous aliens who did not leave voluntarily, Pickering wanted to apply the full force of the law, but to some degree he was frustrated by Adams, who was unwilling to cede control over either the law's interpretation or its execution. At the end of the congressional session in July 1798, Adams quickly decamped from Philadelphia to his home in Quincy, Massachusetts. He remained there, nursing his critically ill wife, Abigail, until he absolutely had to leave to attend the December 3 beginning of Congress, and he left again soon after Congress adjourned in March. Adams mostly governed from afar from July 1798 until fall 1799. Adams's cabinet secretaries who remained in Philadelphia regularly sent dispatches to Quincy and received directives in return. In October 1798, Pickering sent Adams some blank deportation orders. In part, he sought approval for a standard form, while also seeking the authority to fill out the orders himself in consultation with the other department heads in Adams's absence. Adams swiftly dismissed the idea, writing, "I think, we ought to give the act a strict construction, and therefore doubt the propriety of delegating the authority."[9] Adams decided to keep the authority for himself and not let his Francophobic secretary pursue aliens unchecked.

About the same time, Adams did agree to issue deportation orders for three people, including Georges-Henri-Victor Collot, a French general who was connected to a plot to separate Louisiana from Spain and part of the western United States from America. These men seemed to be just the kind of people the Alien Friends Act was meant to target. Pickering, however, did not immediately implement the orders. Instead, he arranged for the men to be watched in the hopes of collecting evidence against other suspicious aliens.[10] Nearly a year later, Pickering updated Adams and admitted that "when other business pressed, the pursuit of these aliens was overlooked."[11] Perhaps it was not simply Pickering's incompetence that allowed Collot to remain in the United States, but a concern that Collot possessed too much information and expert knowledge about the southwestern frontier for him to be safely returned to France. For if France was truly planning an invasion or a military mission to retake the Louisiana Territory from Spain, Collot could have provided valuable intelligence. Because Collot was officially a British prisoner, having been arrested by Spain while in New Orleans and paroled to the United States, Pickering arranged with the British minister to drag out negotiations for a prisoner exchange including Collot. Collot remained safely under the Americans' watch until he returned to France in late 1800.[12] With Collot unable to leave the United States, Pickering identified other targets for deportation. In that same letter to Adams, Pickering suggested using the Alien Friends Act against Cooper, to which Adams agreed. Unfortunately, it was too late because Cooper had already become a citizen. Eventually, these suspicious aliens and others left the United States on their own, without the government having to take any action.

Adams did consider using the Alien Friends Law against one Federalist editor, Englishman William Cobbett, who published *Porcupine's Gazette*. Cobbett's paper was routinely filled with vitriolic attacks against Democratic-Republicans, but after Adams reopened negotiations with France in the winter of 1799, Cobbett turned all his scorn against Adams. Cobbett expressed nothing but disdain for the prospect of the new mission and predicted that Adams's nominations would be "instantaneously followed by the loss of every friend worth his preserving." The next day, he accused Adams of being "deluded and deceived."[13] Although Adams believed Cobbett should be deported, he never pursued it, probably because he knew that Pickering agreed with Cobbett and would not have supported his deportation. Cobbett voluntarily returned to England in June 1800.[14] By the time the Alien Friends Act expired on June 25, 1800, Adams and Pickering had considered deporting only a handful of aliens. They never actually deported anyone.

—

Federalist leaders possessed no such qualms about implementing the Sedition Act. Even before the law's passage, Federalists pursued three seditious libel cases under common law, that is, judge-made as opposed to written statute law. One case that did not result in formal indictment is significant because it involved a member of Congress and his routine communications with his constituents. During the debates on the Sedition Act in 1798, Federalist representatives attacked their Democratic-Republican colleagues on several occasions for spreading lies and encouraging opposition to the government. The case against a Democratic-Republican congressman from Albemarle, Virginia, was the Federalists' first attempt to curb representatives' speech. In May 1797, a federal grand jury in Richmond, Virginia, recommended that Joseph Cabell be charged with seditious libel for the contents of a circular letter to his constituents. The grand jury accused Cabell of attacking the government in a time of "real public danger" and spreading "unfounded calumnies against the happy government of the United States." The grand jury charged that Cabell's purpose had been to separate the people from the government and "to increase or produce foreign influence, ruinous to the peace, happiness, and independence of the United States."[15] Cabell was never formally indicted, and the incident petered out. Federalists failed in their attempt to censure Cabell for engaging in the standard practice of circulating news about what he and Congress had done during the latest session. The incident did alert Thomas Jefferson and others to the Federalist designs and what they saw as potential abuse of the judicial system by the government in power. Jefferson believed that the best way to prevent such misuse of power was to ensure that federal juries reflected the local community by being elected rather than appointed by the federal marshal. Jefferson deplored what he called the "foreign influence" of the federal government and asserted that states should maintain control over their own citizens. The Virginia House of Delegates criticized the presentment as a "violation of fundamental principles of representation . . . an usurpation of power . . . and a subjection of a natural right of speaking and writing freely." Jefferson and the Virginia legislature foreshadowed their arguments against the Alien and Sedition Acts in their response to the grand jury's actions.[16]

The first successful common-law indictment for seditious libel was against Bache. In June, while Congress debated the alien and sedition bills, Bache again provoked the administration by printing a letter from the French foreign minister before Adams had even informed Congress of its arrival. Shortly thereafter, Bache was indicted for seditious libel against the president and the executive branch under common law. He appeared in court, posted bail, and received a trial date for the October session.[17] A month before his trial, Bache died, a victim of a yellow fever epidemic. Federalists never received complete satisfaction against him. Much to their chagrin, his newspaper and all its vehement anti-Federalism lived on as his widow along with employee William Duane continued publishing.

The Federalists had much more success against John Daly Burk, who was indicted on July 6, only a week before the Sedition Act passed. Burk edited the *Time-Piece*, the most radical paper in New York. In 1796, Burk had fled Ireland, where he had organized revolutionary cells, under the threat of arrest for sedition. Burk, like other immigrants, imagined America to be a place where he would find true freedom. The Alien and Sedition Acts proved him wrong. In the time that he edited the paper, Burk kept up a steady attack against Adams's policies and defended free speech. In the face of regular street fights between Federalists and Democratic-Republicans, Burk hired seventy men to protect his presses. The district attorney, with a little prompting from Pickering, arrested Burk on the charge of "seditious and libelous" writing against the president, and had Burk's business partner indicted for defamatory libel. Both men were released on bail pending trial. Federalists were pleased, but Burk continued to write without restraint. His partner refused to follow Burk and distanced himself from Burk's enterprise. Within a month the partnership was dissolved, and by September the *Time-Piece* ceased to exist. The Federalist press celebrated, wishing a similar fate for every Democratic-Republican paper. With the paper's demise, prosecutors decided to drop the charges against Burk because he promised to leave the country. Burk never left, but settled quietly in Virginia, where he waited for the Alien and Sedition Acts to expire.[18]

Finally, Federalists moved against William Durrell, editor of the *Mount Pleasant Register*. Durrell was not arrested until a couple weeks after the Sedition Act had passed, but he seems to have been arrested under common law for a paragraph he had reprinted from another newspaper critical of the government in June. Unlike Bache and Burk, Durrell did not want to risk accidently offending Federalist authorities and so immediately shut down his paper. Although Durrell was free on bail, he had essentially given up his livelihood while waiting to be formally indicted and brought to trial. In fact, he had to wait a long time. He was not indicted until fall 1799, and his trial did not take place until spring 1800. Meanwhile, his property was foreclosed upon and he could barely support his wife and five children. At his trial, Durrell apologized for his actions, although not for the content of the piece he reprinted. Not surprisingly, he was convicted and sentenced to four months in jail. Unlike any of the others convicted of sedition, Durrell was granted a partial pardon by Adams. After only two weeks in jail, he was released on the condition that he post a $2,000 bond for good behavior—a part of his original sentence.[19] Federalists had limited success with common-law prosecutions, and so they hoped that the Sedition Act would be more effective.

Although Federalists won all the sedition cases they brought to trial, they did not win the battle for the hearts and minds of the American people, and they certainly did not successfully silence their critics. Instead, the trials proved to be a near-perfect forum for the accused to show how little regard Federalists had for the rights of speech and the press or for fair trials. The Federalist judges acted more as prosecutors than judges, which only seemed to aid Democratic-Republican defendants in becoming political martyrs to the cause of freedom.

Congressman Matthew Lyon of Vermont, who had long been the target of Federalist scorn, was the first to be charged under the Sedition Act. Lyon arrived in America in 1764 from Ireland as an indentured servant. He was a political and economic outsider who was able to amass wealth through his ambition and entrepreneurial skill. He speculated in land, built mills, engaged in various manufacturing enterprises, and infamously established several newspapers. Nevertheless, he had to fight hard to gain a foothold in Vermont and national politics. It took him three tries to get elected to the House. In that last election, he effectively used his newspaper as a political weapon. Lyon was the first printer to serve in the House. There he scandalously got into a bloody fight with a Federalist congressman from Connecticut on the House floor only six months before the Sedition Act passed.[20] Three months after the law passed, Lyon was arrested at his home in Vermont for wickedly and maliciously contriving to defame the government and president.[21] There were three specific counts against him. In the first, the government charged that a letter written by Lyon and published in *Spooner's Vermont Journal* was seditious libel against Adams. The second and third counts related to Lyon's use of a letter by an American expatriate in Paris who took part in the French Revolution. Lyon read the letter at his campaign events and published it.[22]

Unlike many of his fellow Sedition Act defendants, Lyon elected to have an immediate trial. Then he chose to represent himself when bad weather delayed his lawyers. Lyon made three points in his defense. First, the Sedition Act was unconstitutional and void. Furthermore, although Lyon's letter was published after the law was enacted, Lyon had written the letter before

"Congressional Pugilists," Philadelphia, 1798. Verbal sparring in the House of Representatives between Federalist Roger Griswold of Connecticut (*right*) and Democratic-Republican Matthew Lyon of Vermont (*left*) erupted into violence, while the nation waited for news of the first mission to France during the winter of 1798. This fracas was just one manifestation of the tensions and conflicts among government officials, political parties, and the American people about public policy and the nation's character. *Source:* Library of Congress, Washington, DC

passage. When it was written should determine whether the contents were subject to the law, Lyon argued, not when it was published. Second, he had no malicious intent and thus did not violate the law. And third, the content of the letters was true. Lyon took full advantage of his trial not to make legal points but political ones. In the letter, Lyon condemned Adams for sacrificing the public welfare and grasping power "in an unbounded thirst for ridiculous pomp, foolish adulation, and selfish avarice." Lyon's defense hinged on calling as a witness the presiding judge, Associate Justice William Paterson, to prove the truth of part of the allegedly seditious letter. Although Paterson refused to be a formal witness, Lyon engaged Paterson in an exchange about

Adams's conduct. Lyon asked whether Paterson had "dined with the President, and observed his ridiculous pomp and parade?" Paterson answered that when he dined with the president he never saw pomp and parade but "a great deal of plainness and simplicity." Lyon then asked whether Paterson had seen more pomp and servants at the seat of government than in Rutland, Vermont, where the trial took place. Paterson declined to answer, as his response would have been favorable to Lyon. There was no comparison between rural Vermont and cosmopolitan Philadelphia. Lyon called no other witnesses.

After closing statements from both sides, Paterson gave his instructions to the jury. Like Lyon's defense, these instructions were as much a political statement as legal guidance for the jury. Paterson declared that juries could not decide a law's constitutionality. The only issues for them to decide were whether Lyon published the letters and whether those letters were seditious. Lyon readily admitted publication. As to the second question, the jury had to decide whether Lyon published the material with "any other intent than that of making odious or contemptible the President and government, and bringing them both into disrepute." After deliberating for an hour, the jury returned a guilty verdict. In sentencing Lyon, Paterson admonished him for not recognizing "the mischiefs which flow from an unlicensed abuse of government . . . No one, also, can be better acquainted than yourself with the existence and nature of the act." Paterson sentenced Lyon to four months in jail and a $1,000 fine plus court costs.

While Federalists everywhere rejoiced at Lyon's conviction, jail did not effectively silence him. With his son as the publisher, Lyon established a new magazine called *The Scourge of Aristocracy and Repository of Important Political Truths*. His letters included the dateline "In jail at Vergennes," a constant reminder to his readers of where he was. Lyon told his story through his magazine and in a printed and widely circulated letter addressed to Virginia Senator Stevens T. Mason. With this public letter, Lyon framed his ordeal as a political witch hunt. He would later put his trial and conviction at the center of his reelection campaign, becoming the first congressman to run for and win reelection while in prison. In January 1799, the ever-defiant Lyon addressed his constituents and thanked them for their support. He referenced the previous months' debate by saying his reelection resembled the "truly noble and generous efforts of the Patriots of Virginia and Kentucky, in holding up to abhorence [sic] Tyranny, and unconstitutional Laws." By reelecting him, Vermont voters announced "that their confidence in the Representative is unabated; and that to his care and integrity they choose to consign their national interests, for more than two years to come."[23] Still, he could not attend Congress until he completed his sentence and paid his fine.

In February 1799, Mason traveled to Vermont to personally pay Lyon's fine in gold. Thomas Jefferson, James Madison, James Monroe, Albert Gallatin, and other leading Democratic-Republicans also contributed to Lyon's cause. In addition, Lyon's constituents collected $1,000 in silver, but they deferred to Mason and let him pay the fine. Upon leaving jail, Lyon declared that he was on his way to Congress, claiming the immunity from prosecution given to all elected officials while engaged in official business. Crowds and parades triumphantly accompanied him on his way to Philadelphia. Still, Lyon's ordeal was not over. His conviction remained a political issue. Even before he arrived in Philadelphia, efforts were under way to expel him from Congress. Pro-expulsion Federalists stressed the danger Lyon posed to the republic. Democratic-Republicans emphasized Vermonters' right to freely choose their own representative. Federalists failed to win the two-thirds majority needed to expel a member and Lyon quietly served out the rest of his term, but his fame reached well beyond Vermont and Congress. The Democratic-Republican press made Lyon a hero in the cause of liberty. A typical toast to Lyon cheered him as a "martyr to the cause of Liberty and the Rights of Man: may his sufferings bring good out of evil, by arousing the people to guard their rights and oppose every unconstitutional measure."[24]

—

Like Lyon, Cooper exploited the Sedition Act for political purposes. Unlike others, he invited arrest by not using a pseudonym and publicizing his work. When he was arrested, Cooper knew that he would be convicted. He then published his own account of the trial within weeks of its conclusion during the height of the presidential campaign. Cooper had been politically active in his native England and in fact had come to the United States with the intention of founding a settlement for English dissenters. When that plan failed, he settled about 150 miles northwest of Philadelphia in Northumberland, Pennsylvania, where his fellow chemist and English political refugee, Joseph Priestly, resided with his family. In America, he tried his hand at farming, and when that failed turned to law and politics. When the Alien and Sedition Acts passed, Cooper became a citizen and intensified his political activity. He served as editor of the *Northumberland Gazette* from April through June 1799 and immediately earned the attention of Federalists when he wrote a series of essays critical of Adams. Duane reprinted Cooper's essays in the *Aurora* that summer. Two editions of Cooper's *Political Essays* were printed in 1799 and 1800. In turn, Cooper represented Duane when the Senate accused Duane of sedition and breach of privilege. Even though Cooper's allegedly seditious pieces had been published months before, it was only after the Senate charged Duane with contempt that Cooper was indicted. At the time of his arrest, Cooper was not directly connected with a newspaper, but was rather fully engaged in politics.[25]

The basis of the case against Cooper was his failed solicitation of a federal government job when Adams first assumed the presidency. Federalists accused Cooper of being a political opportunist. Cooper defended himself and in doing so attacked Adams, maintaining that there was no impropriety in his actions because Adams "was hardly in the infancy of political mistake." Thus it was not Cooper but Adams who had betrayed his political principles. Cooper then listed the misguided policies Adams had enacted during his first years in office. Nearly five months after this article was published, Cooper was indicted.[26] Federalists portrayed him as a disgruntled office seeker and a political chameleon. Like Lyon, Cooper opted not to delay his trial. He was arrested, charged, and tried in April 1800.

Cooper's trial took place in Philadelphia, and Associate Justice Samuel Chase presided with Federal District Judge Richard Peters. Marylander Chase had signed the Declaration of Independence and had been an active member of the Continental Congress during the Revolution. He had opposed the ratification of the Constitution, but by the time President George Washington nominated him to the Supreme Court in 1795, he was a staunch Federalist. Ultra Federalists probably had no better friend on the court than Chase when it came to defending the Sedition Act. Chase, however, invited controversy in almost every office in which he served. He resigned from the Continental Congress in 1778 amid charges of corruption. Then, when serving as Maryland's chief judge, he was accused of abusing his power. Although nothing came of these charges, similar complaints would be made against him as an associate justice, and in 1804 he was impeached by House Democratic-Republicans. The Senate could not muster the two-thirds majority to convict him; a much tamer Chase remained in office until his death in 1811. Impeachment resulted from three trials that Chase presided over in a period of a few months in the spring and early summer of 1800: two for sedition (Cooper and

Callender) and one for treason (John Fries). After these trials, Democratic-Republicans started calling Chase "the hanging judge."[27]

Cooper's trial was a noteworthy event in Philadelphia. Pickering, the secretaries of war and the Navy, and Adams's private secretary attended. Representative Robert Goodloe Harper, who was instrumental in passing and defending the Sedition Act, also regularly attended. In addition, Federalist senators Uriah Tracy of Connecticut and James Ross of Pennsylvania, who were both deeply involved in the Senate's conflict with Duane and thus Cooper, were present.[28] Among the Democratic-Republicans present was Alexander J. Dallas, who had defended Duane in his trial for seditious riot. Cooper, like Lyon, defended himself. Cooper's decision to represent himself is another sign that he sought to make his trial a political event, not just a legal one. He retained control over the tone and direction of the defense. Cooper decided his main defense would be truth. In order to prove it, Cooper needed the testimony of government officials, including some of the spectators, and the president. When arraigned, Cooper requested that Adams and Pickering, among others, be subpoenaed.

With Pickering sitting a few yards away, the issue of subpoenas focused only on whether a sitting president could be called to testify. Cooper argued that he did not voluntarily write the offending piece, but was forced to defend himself after the president had disclosed information from what Cooper believed was private correspondence. He said, "I was first compelled to appear before the public, and am now dragged into this court to vindicate my character against anonymous slander and legal accusation." Furthermore, in a republic, Cooper argued, no one should be considered above the law, including the president. Chase, as he did throughout the trial, challenged every defense argument. He rejected Cooper's "very improper and a very indecent request" because he argued the president could not be compelled to appear in libel cases. Moreover, Chase could not fathom questioning the president on whether he was "guilty of maladministration." Having been denied the right to directly question Adams, Cooper sought to submit other evidence of Adams's policy mistakes, including copies of his annual message as published in the newspapers. In response, the government's attorney, William Rawle, with Chase's full support, successfully argued that these newspaper accounts were not the originals and thus could not be submitted as evidence. Chase set an impossibly high bar for proving the truth.

Rawle readily admitted that the government hoped to make Cooper an example. In his closing argument he stated, "It was a sense of public duty that called for this prosecution. . . . an example should be made to deter others from misleading the people by such false and defamatory publications." He reiterated that the government had the right and duty to punish seditious speech in order to protect itself and the nation. Publications like Cooper's were dangerous because "Error leads to discontent, discontent to a fancied idea of oppression, and that to insurrection, of which the two instances which had already happened, were alarming proofs, and well known to the jury."*

Cooper, unable to present any substantive evidence of truth, closed with a political speech against the Sedition Act and the dangers of limiting speech. He proclaimed the government was free to do whatever it wanted "While those who venture to express a sentiment of opposition must do it in fear and trembling, and run the hazard of being dragged like myself before the frowning tribunal, erected by the Sedition Law." Cooper believed that opinion was "better confuted by evidence and argument than by indictment—Fines and imprisonment, will produce conviction neither in the mind of the sufferer, nor of the public." He used his trial as a forum for his political views.

Like Cooper, Chase used the trial to make a political statement in the guise of instructions to the jury. First, Chase told the jury they had to decide who wrote the allegedly seditious piece, to which Cooper had already confessed. The second question was whether Cooper exhibited "bad intent." Chase explained to the jury that the burden of proof rested with the defendant, meaning effectively that Cooper was guilty until he could prove himself innocent. The justice emphasized the falsehoods present in Cooper's writings, which placed the republic in danger by undermining the people's confidence. Chase said, "If a man attempts to destroy the confidence of the people in their officers, their supreme magistrate, and their legislature, he effectually saps the foundation of the government." For Chase, elections were the proper forum for the people to express their beliefs. Cooper's publications were thus the "boldest attempt . . . to poison the minds of the people." Chase then sent the case to the jury. Not surprisingly, the jury found Cooper guilty, and Chase sentenced Cooper to six months in prison and a $400 fine. Of the trial, Senator Mason told Madison that "A more oppressiv[e] and disgusting proceeding I never saw. Chase in his charge to the Jury (in a speech of an hour) shewed

---

* The two instances were the Whiskey and Fries's Rebellions.

all the zeal of a well fee'd Lawyer and the rancour of a vindictive and implacable enemy."[29] Both Chase and Cooper used the trial to make political points, seemingly at the expense of legal arguments.

As with Lyon, prison did not silence Cooper. A week after he was sentenced, Cooper printed an account of his trial. In the preface, Cooper explained that if people wished to avoid persecution, "they will hold their tongues, and restrain their pens, on the subject of politics: at least during the continuance of the SEDITION LAW." Because, under the law, "the plainest truths, and the most notorious facts, may be converted and denied; and the innocent and well-meaning asserter of them, may be driven with impunity, to spend his time and exhaust his finances, in procuring proof strictly legal of what no man in common life pretends to doubt."[30] Although Adams initially endorsed the prosecution, after the trial he believed the prosecutors had gone too far. To make amends, he offered Cooper a pardon only if Cooper would request one. Cooper refused and served his full sentence. He fully embraced the role of martyr to the cause of freedom of the press.

After Chase dispensed with Cooper, he went to Richmond, where he would preside over the only sedition trial in the South—that of James Thomson Callender. Virginia Governor James Monroe had predicted that the Federalists would attempt to prove the Sedition Act was operative in Virginia sometime during the summer of 1800. He saw it as "an electioneering trick."[31] Callender was the obvious target for Federalists. Callender had been born in Scotland and lived on the edge economically, socially, and politically. A job with the British government had exposed him to the corruption both real and perceived that he would fight for the rest of his life. In 1792, he published a pamphlet in which he attacked the British government. His biographer characterizes the pamphlet as "one of the most inflammatory, undeferential, and militant texts to be published in the 1790s."[32] At the risk of arrest for sedition in England, Callender fled to America, where he continued his career as a journalist and political hack. Even in the United States, Callender remained on the fringes of society. He was once thrown out of the halls of Congress for being "covered with lice and filth" and probably drunk as well.[33] The Federalist *Porcupine's Gazette* characterized Callender as "a little reptile" and "a nasty beast."[34] But Callender was a talented writer and adept at the kind of political invective that could rile opponents. He found enough financial support from Democratic-Republicans, including Jefferson, to continue his pamphleteering career. In 1798, Callender faced both professional and personal challenges. His wife died, and he had to care for his children while facing political prosecution under the Sedition Act. Like Cooper, he became a citizen to avoid deportation under the Alien Friends Act. Leaving his children in Philadelphia, he went to Virginia, where he found refuge with Mason, who had given material and political aid to Lyon. Callender stayed at Mason's plantation for several months before attempting to reestablish his political propagandist career. He eventually landed a position with the *Richmond Examiner*. In 1800, he penned *The Prospect Before Us*, a multivolume work promoting Jefferson's candidacy in which he called Adams a "hoary headed incendiary."[35]

Interestingly, Chase initiated the case against Callender when he received a copy of *The Prospect Before Us* after arriving in Richmond. Shortly thereafter, the grand jury indicted Callender, and his trial began despite pleas from his lawyers for a delay. Callender had able defense lawyers in George Hay, who authored an anti–Alien and Sedition Acts pamphlet; Philip Norborne Nicholas, from a prominent Democratic-Republican family; and William Wirt, who was a transplant to Virginia and a staunch Democratic-Republican. Their task was almost impossible, as they faced not only Chase but also an all-Federalist jury.[36] Callender's defense sought to show that a distinction could not be made between fact and opinion. Hay asked what evidence was necessary to prove "that the reign of Mr. Adams has been one continued tempest of malignant passions?" As to some of Adams's alleged statements, Hay argued that some men could find that these words were of "passion and malignity," while others could believe Adams "spoke the plain truth." Opinion could be the subject of endless discussion. Hay implied that no evidence could prove the truth of Callender's statements because the truth of an opinion could never be fully proven. Not surprisingly, Chase inserted himself into the argument. Chase dismissed the defense's arguments as a waste of time. He proclaimed that Callender charged Adams with being "a murderer and a thief, a despot and a tyrant! Will you call a man a murderer and a thief, and excuse yourself by saying it is but mere opinion—or, that you heard so?" For Chase, the only question was that of Callender's intent, and that was for the jury to decide.

The Federalist district attorney tried to use the trials to show the danger of the Democratic-Republicans' ideal of the absolute freedom of the press. The government acknowledged citizens' right to choose their rulers at each election, but that right, he argued, "does not warrant him to vilify, revile, and defame another individual, who is a candidate." The Federalist prosecutor con demned the practice of proving the worth of one candidate by insulting the other. "The whole forms a perfect chain of malice, falsehood, and slander." And, Federalists argued, this practice would ultimately destroy the Union.

Already hobbled by not being allowed to argue the difference between fact and opinion and not having the time to mount a thorough defense, Callender's lawyers also faced Chase's mercurial behavior. Chase frequently interrupted and imposed requirements upon them that he did not require of the prosecution. For example, Chase demanded that the defense submit their questions for one witness in writing. When Nicholas objected, Chase ruled that the jury could hear only legal evidence and he wanted to ensure that the questioning adhered to this standard. Chase then ruled the witness's testimony inadmissible because it spoke to only part of the charges and not the whole. While the defense was up in arms over the ruling, Chase evoked the power of his office. He stated, "My country has made me a judge, and you must be governed now by my opinion." Chase effectively prevented the defense from presenting the case as they had wanted.

The defense changed tactics once again, this time focusing their arguments on the unconstitutionality of the law. Because the jury could decide both law and fact, they argued, the jury could rule on the law's constitutionality. Paterson had rejected this argument as dangerous and untenable in Lyon's trial, and Chase did the same in Callender's, although with a few more fireworks. During an exchange on this point, Chase ordered Wirt to sit down and be quiet. Then Chase interrupted Hay, at which point Hay had had enough and simply refused to continue. Callender's defense rested. His attorneys certainly took advantage of Chase's reputation and temper to make the political point that a fair trial was impossible. With an all-Federalist jury, it was unlikely that Callender would have been acquitted. Political points were more important than legal ones.

Chase predictably made his own political points in his charge to the jury. For Chase, the government had to prove that Callender wrote the matter in question, and the government ably did so. Second, the jury had to decide whether the writing was false, scandalous, and malicious. Finally, the jury had to determine whether the material was published with the intent to defame. The authority of the jury to decide fact and law meant that juries interpreted the law before them, not the law's constitutionality. That power belonged solely to the federal judiciary as the "only proper and competent authority to decide whether any statute made by Congress (or any of the state legislatures) is contrary to, or in violation of, the Federal Constitution." Otherwise, juries would be made superior to Congress, and federal law potentially would have been operative in one state and not another. With this one statement, Chase dismissed many of the arguments Democratic-Republicans had been making against the Alien and Sedition Acts for the past two years. After two hours of deliberation, the jury found Callender guilty. Chase subsequently sentenced him to nine months in jail and a $200 fine. Before sentencing, Chase could not resist one more lecture. He commended the jury for their verdict, which showed "that the laws of the United States could be enforced in Virginia, the principal object of this prosecution." With Callender's conviction, Chase declared that the national government—and thus Federalist authority—operated in Democratic-Republican Virginia. He censured Callender for spreading "dissensions, discontent, and discord among the people" and for failing to appreciate Adams's service to the nation.

Callender served his time in Richmond, where he complained frequently of the deplorable conditions and company. It was uncomfortably hot in the summer and cold in the winter. He wrote, "Unless a man has the constitution of a horse he must in such lodgings either catch his death of cold, or think himself happy in escaping with a rooted rheumatism." In September, he had to share his quarters with prisoners from the failed slave insurrection led by Gabriel Prosser. Although Callender opposed slavery when he arrived in America, after living in Virginia for eighteen months, his attitudes had changed and were more in line with the Virginians for whom he worked. He endorsed hanging the conspirators and generally disdained having to live in close quarters with blacks. Local Democratic-Republicans did not wholly abandon him after his trial. Mason, Taylor, Jefferson, members of the Virginia legislature, and others contributed money to his defense, fine, and board in prison. Monroe and others visited Callender in prison, and his jailer—a protégé of Jefferson's—granted Callender some special privileges, like spending time in the prison yard; these small pleasures were stopped only after local Federalists complained to the federal marshal.

As with Lyon and Cooper, jail did not prevent Callender from writing critical pieces about Adams and the Federalists. He continued to send drafts to Jefferson. Before his trial and the presidential campaign, Jefferson regularly responded to Callender and paid him for his writings. Significantly, after Callender's conviction, Jefferson stopped commenting on Callender's drafts. When Callender returned to his previous practice of vitriolic scandalmongering and political attacks, the support of now-moderate and respectable Virginia Democratic-Republicans faded away. After Jefferson's election as president, Callender, whose financial situation always seemed desperate, assumed that he would be awarded with a patronage job, but he received no offers. In fact, Monroe advised Jefferson in the summer of 1801 to end his relationship with Callender "to prevent even a serpent doing one an injury."[37] True enough, after being spurned by Jefferson and his friends, Callender turned his pen against them. Most famously, he exposed Jefferson's affair with his slave Sally Hemings. In July 1803, Callender drowned in Richmond's James River, mostly likely drunk once again.

—

Federalists could not effectively silence Lyon, Cooper, and Callender, but Duane of Philadelphia's *Aurora* proved to be the Federalists' most difficult challenge. Federalist leaders had tried and failed on several different occasions to shut down the paper when edited by Bache, who was only silenced by death during a yellow fever epidemic. Duane proved equally if not more difficult to muzzle. Duane, like Bache, was a victim of physical violence when a mob beat him unconscious. Much to the Federalists' annoyance and embarrassment, he possessed the same uncanny ability to escape Federalists' traps.

Duane was born in America in 1760 but grew up in Ireland and spent time in England and India before returning to the United States in 1796. Along the way, he was expelled from India for praising the French Revolution and escaped prosecution for sedition in England by fleeing on a ship to America. When he arrived in Philadelphia, he was "wretchedly poor and friendless," but he quickly made connections with the Democratic-Republican press and became a leader of the immigrant Irish community. Duane identified himself as a member of the United Irishmen, a group Federalists associated with Jacobinism. In spring 1798, Bache hired Duane to write for the *Aurora*, and in November Duane became the editor. In 1800, he married Bache's widow and continued Bache's mission.[38]

In February 1799, Duane was among the Irish immigrants who organized a petition against the Alien Friends Act. They posted notices at a church that the petition could be signed after services that day in the churchyard. The day ended with a confrontation between those who supported the petition and those who opposed it. One of Duane's companions pulled a gun on their opponents. Duane and two others were arrested for seditious riot, and although it was his companion who escalated the tension, the case became known

William Duane (1780–1865) printed one of the most important and influential
Democratic-Republican newspapers, Philadelphia's *Aurora*, after the death of
Benjamin Franklin Bache in 1798. Federalists tried and failed to convict Duane of
sedition on several occasions. *Source:* Library of Congress, Washington, DC

as "Duane's case." Federalists considered Duane the most important party
even though he had little to do with the actual fracas. The case against the
defendants, especially Duane, was weak. The prosecutor argued that aliens
did not have the right to petition; this right belonged exclusively to citizens.
The defense answered with a spirited vindication of that right for everyone
regardless of citizenship status. After thirty minutes of deliberation, the jury
acquitted Duane and the others.[39] Duane escaped Federalists' first attempt to
silence him.

In July 1799, Pickering recommended using the Alien Friends and Sedition Acts against Duane. Enclosing a copy of that morning's paper with the
offending articles marked, Pickering wrote to Adams, "There is in the Aurora
in this city of uninterrupted stream of slander on the American government."
He continued, "It is not the first time that the editor has suggested, that you
had asserted the influence of the British government in affairs of our own,
and insinuated that it was obtained by bribery." Not only could they charge
Duane with sedition, but he was also a candidate for deportation under the

Alien Friends Act. Although Duane claimed American citizenship, Pickering explained that Duane was born in Vermont when it was a colony and his parents returned to Ireland before the Revolution. Duane did not return to the United States until the 1790s. Furthermore, Duane posed dangers beyond that of publishing a newspaper. Pickering suspected that the militia company made up exclusively of Irish immigrants that Duane had helped found was "probably formed to oppose the authority of the government; and in case of war and invasion by the French, to join them."[40] Adams fully endorsed the effort to go after Duane. He wrote that if the federal attorney "does not think this paper libellous, he is not fit for his office; and if he does not prosecute it, he will not do his duty." In addition, "The matchless effrontery of this Duane merits the execution of the alien law. I am very willing to try its strength upon him."[41] Legal proceedings were quickly initiated against Duane.

On August 2, Duane was arrested and arraigned for sedition. Specifically, Duane was indicted for censuring the government for operating under British influence and accusing officials of taking bribes from the British secret service. Unlike the trials of Lyon, Cooper, and Callender, Duane's was postponed until the next court session in October. Unlike those men, who did not have successful newspapers at the time of their arrest, Duane did not need to make his political points through a public trial. He could do that every day in his paper. In October, Duane's attorney asked for another postponement because witnesses—Pickering, James Monroe, and Tench Coxe—were not available. The court agreed, and his trial was delayed until June 11, 1800. Duane remained free on $3,000 bond. He did not temper his behavior, but instead continued to criticize Federalists relentlessly. Federalists had reason to allow the trial to be postponed twice. Duane stated publicly that he could prove the truth with letters written by Adams, Pickering, and the British minister to the United States, which he had in his possession. In June, the prosecution withdrew the charges precisely because of these letters. They did not indict him again. Duane successfully used truth as his defense—the only defendant to do so—and escaped the second attack against him.[42]

As the sedition prosecution against Duane was unraveling, the Senate took up the challenge. In February 1800, Democratic-Republican senators leaked a copy of a controversial Federalist bill that would have established an all-Federalist election commission to resolve any questions with the upcoming presidential election. Duane criticized both the bill and Federalists' tactics. He characterized Federalists as "the party hostile to the popular interest."[43] Federalist senators were up in arms. Instead of initiating a sedition case against him, the Senate decided to charge Duane with a breach of privilege and contempt of the Senate. The formal charges shared the language of indictments under the Sedition Act. A committee created quasi-judicial procedures to try Duane. Although the committee invited Duane to present a defense, it refused to allow his lawyers, one of whom was Cooper, to present arguments supporting the truth of Duane's statements. Duane believed that he would not get a fair hearing from the Federalist-dominated body and went into hiding instead of honoring the Senate's order. Much to senators' chagrin, Duane managed to continue to edit and print the *Aurora*. When the Senate adjourned in mid-May, it asked Adams to order Duane's arrest for sedition. Adams complied, and federal officials found him. He was indicted on October 17, but his trial was postponed and never happened. Duane escaped Federalists a third and final time. Federalists never successfully made an example of Duane. Instead, he demonstrated time and again how difficult it was for Federalists to silence their critics through the judicial system.

Of the other sedition prosecutions, some were initiated by local Federalist politicians or rival newspapers, and some were the result of a connection to another seditious editor. Anthony Haswell in Vermont, for example, was arrested in October 1799 after printing an advertisement for a lottery to benefit Lyon and reprinting a paragraph from the *Aurora*. Haswell did support Lyon and penned several poems and songs praising him, but he was not singled out for those works. From his arrest until his trial in May 1800, Haswell did not publish his paper in order to focus on preparing his defense. Once convicted and sentenced, Haswell, unlike others, asked Adams for a pardon because he could not financially support his wife and nine children from jail. Adams never responded to Haswell's request. Again, jail did not quiet the seditious libeler or cause the people to abandon the editor. Haswell's neighbors postponed their July 4 celebration until Haswell's release on July 9, when the crowd of 2,000 could triumphantly escort him home.[44]

In another case, Federalists prosecuted a drunken man for making a joke about the president. As Adams passed through Newark, New Jersey, on his way from Philadelphia to Quincy at the end of the congressional session in summer 1798, the community, like many others, honored him. Adams was met by a delegation of local dignitaries and saluted with artillery fired by the Association of Young Men. The group fired their cannon late after the president had passed, about which a drunk Luther Baldwin commented, "There goes the President and they are firing at his a--." Another spectator declared Baldwin's comment seditious. Baldwin's observation was neither sophisticated nor subtle satire, but the utterance of a man who had had a few too many and happened to be a Democratic-Republican. Two months later, when Associate Justice William Cushing arrived to preside over the circuit court session, Baldwin was indicted. What distinguished Baldwin's case from the others was not only that he was prosecuted for something he said, not wrote or printed, but also that he eventually pled guilty. He was fined and received no additional prison sentence, although he was remanded to jail until he paid his fine. Baldwin's case demonstrates how little criticism Federalists tolerated.[45]

—

Finally, the case of David Frothingham and the *Argus*, one of the leading Democratic-Republican newspapers in the country and a target of Adams and Pickering, merits some discussion. When the paper's editors avoided trial in federal courts and continued to publish the paper, Federalists tried using the state courts and common law to silence the *Argus*. They went after Frothingham, a journeyman printer and employee instead of the editor. Thomas Greenleaf, the editor, died from yellow fever in fall 1798 before he could be tried for sedition. Like Bache's widow, Greenleaf's widow, Ann, took over the business. The New York district attorney consequently charged Ann Greenleaf with sedition for stating that the "federal Government was corrupt and inimical to the preservation of Liberty." Her trial, like others, was postponed until April 1800 because she herself fell ill with yellow fever.[46]

 Perhaps frustrated by the slow pace of the federal prosecution or to test a more expansive definition of "seditious practices," Alexander Hamilton initiated charges against the *Argus* in state court for printing a piece accusing Hamilton of conspiring to buy the *Aurora* in order to silence it. Hamilton believed that by punishing "seditious practices" broadly defined, the government could "preserve confidence in officers of the general government." In order for that confidence to be preserved, Hamilton contended that a sedition law should protect not only the government as a whole but also the reputation and character of public officials. When officials arrived at the *Argus*, Frothingham took responsibility for printing the piece assaulting Hamilton's character, which had first appeared in Boston's *Constitutional Telegraph*. Perhaps he assumed that he would not be the first journeyman printer to be convicted of sedition and wanted to protect Greenleaf, who had already been indicted under the federal law. He was wrong; upon conviction, he was sentenced to four months in jail and a $500 fine, an enormous sum for a man who made just $8 per week.

Although Hamilton did not personally try the case, he certainly advised the prosecutors. Because Frothingham's prosecution was a common-law prosecution and not a federal sedition case, he did not enjoy the limited protections of the federal law of using truth as a defense or allowing the jury to decide questions of both fact and law. The presiding judge limited the jury to a "special verdict," which meant they could rule only on the fact of publication, which no one denied. Hamilton believed that the *Argus* and other papers like it constituted enough of a threat to the confidence of the people that all legal means should be used to silence them. If the federal sedition law was not adequate, state law or common law should be used.

—

Federalists did not successfully implement their vision of the republic and the people's role in it through the enforcement of the Alien and Sedition Acts. Because of discomfort with the Alien Friends Act's provisions and Pickering's indecision and poor administrative skills, no one was ever deported under the law, and few people were effectively monitored. Federalists did intimidate some immigrants enough for them to leave the United States simply because of the threat the law created. Under the Sedition Law, Federalists targeted certain newspapers and editors. They sought to make examples of the most influential editors. Federalists failed to silence Democratic-Republicans, as most of these editors continued to produce antigovernment pieces or publish their newspapers. They used their trials and even indictments for political purposes. Federalists, too, tried to exploit the trials to further their own vision for the republic. The judges who presided over the trials, particularly Chase, often seemed arbitrary and not impartial jurists to the defendants and Democratic-Republicans. Yet these federal judges believed that they acted correctly. They believed the Sedition Law to be constitutional and acted to uphold it. Many of these trials took place in the politically charged atmosphere of a presidential campaign—an election about opposing visions of the proper role of the people in a republic.

5 Equal and Opposite Reaction

WHEN THE SEDITION BILL passed the House of Representatives, Benjamin Franklin Bache issued a warning in his newspaper, the *Aurora*, that "the good citizens of these states had better hold their tongues and make tooth picks of their pens."[1] Democratic-Republican editors throughout the country reprinted his words. This editorial declaration was neither the first nor last time that the *Aurora* challenged Federalist policies. In fact, public agitation against the Alien and Sedition Acts began well before their passage in June and July of 1798 and subsequent arrests and trials for sedition. The public expressed its opinions through newspapers, pamphlets, petition campaigns, public meetings, and state legislatures, as well as in the streets, where verbal attacks occasionally gave way to physical violence. Federalists had attempted to define the proper role of the people in a republic and to identify by law who the people were. Democratic-Republicans contended that the laws went too far and that the Federalist program fundamentally altered the nature of the republic. Democratic-Republicans and their allies feared a loss of liberty and the introduction of tyranny. Federalists feared tyranny, too, but not from the government. Rather, they feared tyranny from foreign nations working through the people.

The debate ebbed and flowed as it ran its course from summer 1798 through the Election of 1800. Federalists and Democratic-Republicans did not sustain the debate with a consistent intensity. Newspapers and pamphlets were constants. Public meetings, resolutions, and petitions peaked during the summer and early fall of 1798. When these meetings did not produce immediate results, Democratic-Republicans turned to the state legislatures, and both Democratic-Republican- and Federalist-controlled legislatures weighed in on the issues. Congress next responded to the public tumult during their session in the winter of 1798–99, when petitioning against the laws surged again. As both parties believed that the future of the republic was at stake, they were willing to try almost anything to win or prove public support.

—

Even the idea of the Alien and Sedition Acts was enough to make some citizens and aliens alter their behavior. Politicians emerging from the charged atmosphere of the late 1790s were often more moderate in public than their pre–1798 public selves. Thomas Jefferson and James Madison exercised great caution about how, where, and with whom they communicated, or they hid their actions from the public by either writing under pseudonyms or having others present their work to the public with the promise not to reveal the authors' identities. Federalists did succeed in labeling some of the more radical Democratic-Republicans and their ideas as un-American and thus illegitimate. They succeeded in moderating some people's views.[2] Nevertheless, despite fears about running afoul of the law, many Democratic-Republicans— leaders and rank-and-file as well—did not and could not remain quiet.

Anyone who had access to a newspaper could have read the congressional debates, countless articles and editorials, and accounts of public meetings. These people would have been familiar with the arguments both for and against the Alien and Sedition Acts. Newspapers regularly reprinted items from other papers. This practice was what made Bache and his successor at the *Aurora*, William Duane, so dangerous to Federalists, as their invectives and insults were widely reprinted in Democratic-Republican newspapers throughout the country. Their influence reached well beyond Philadelphia. The same was true of Federalist papers, although their newspaper network was not as extensive. Pamphlets were also broadly distributed and available beyond the cities in which they were originally printed. For example, Vice President Jefferson asked his friends in Virginia to send him anti–Alien and Sedition Acts pamphlets so he could send them home with Democratic-

Republican congressmen when they left the capital. Thus pamphlets and newspaper articles—whether opinion pieces or accounts of public meetings, protests, or riots—could have a national impact as they circulated throughout the country.

The irony of the Sedition Act was that the number of Democratic-Republican papers actually increased as a result of the law. Federalists succeeded in making the press more partisan—and more Democratic-Republican—rather than less so. By Jefferson's inauguration in March 1801, there was at least one Democratic-Republican paper in every major city and in many small towns. Nearly fifty Democratic-Republican papers were founded after passage of the Sedition Law, compared to about half that number in the two years before its passage. The Sedition Act forced editors to choose sides, and, unfortunately for Federalists, most chose the Democratic-Republicans, whose fortunes although seemingly dismal in 1798 improved as the Election of 1800 approached.[3]

Even though their fortunes faded, Federalists began from a position of strength, and they believed they had the public's support. After passage of the laws in the summer of 1798 and through early 1799, they successfully rebuffed Democratic-Republican attacks. They increased their majority in the House of Representatives and gained seats in several state legislatures in elections in late 1798 and early 1799. But as Democratic-Republicans changed tactics, Federalists proved to be less nimble than their opponents. And then, when President John Adams decided to send a second mission to France in February 1799, Federalists lost their main argument: the imminent danger of a French invasion or an escalation of hostilities and a formal declaration of war with France. With the prospect for peace, however remote, Federalist arguments lost their urgency. Federalists were divided over the new French mission, and those differences played out publicly. As the presidential election approached, Federalist politicians seemed to fight more among themselves than with Democratic-Republicans.

More so than Federalists, Democratic-Republicans successfully changed tactics throughout the debates. Over the summer of 1798, there were numerous public meetings in several states, most notably Kentucky. When these meetings failed to have an immediate impact on the government, Democratic-Republicans organized petition campaigns, and as the fall meetings of the state legislatures approached, they decided to use these institutions as vehicles of protest. The result was the Virginia and Kentucky Resolutions, drafted by Madison and Jefferson, respectively, which were among the most famous and discussed protests against the laws.* The resolutions generated a backlash against the Democratic-Republican cause—not just for their case against the Alien and Sedition Acts but also for their use of the state legislatures. When ten states condemned Virginia and Kentucky's actions, Democratic-Republicans again had to adjust their tactics and arguments. They renewed their efforts to generate anti–Alien and Sedition Acts petitions during the congressional session in the winter of 1798–99. When this effort failed to win the laws' repeal, they turned their attention to the 1800 elections.

—

During the summer of 1798, Democratic-Republican leaders began to mobilize opposition to the laws through public meetings that approved resolutions protesting Federalist policies. Over 4,000 people attended one meeting in Lexington, Kentucky. Just like the efforts surrounding the controversial Neutrality Proclamation and the Jay Treaty, opponents of the Alien and Sedition Acts tried to rally the people and prove that they had public opinion on their side. Accounts of these meetings and the resulting resolutions were widely printed and reprinted in newspapers throughout the country. The Democratic-Republican press praised the protesters' bravery and adherence to the ideals of the American Revolution; the Federalist press responded by characterizing the protests as illegitimate. In *Porcupine's Gazette*, for example, William Cobbett used his typical vitriolic style to refer to those who attended a Kentucky meeting as mobs and hordes, although such monikers could have been applied to any number of meetings. He called the resolutions "barbarous" and the attendees savages who were "just civilized enough to be the tools of faction, and that's all." Democratic-Republican papers, on the other hand, extolled the virtues of the people who attended the meetings and celebrated the communities who were brave enough to protest the laws as bastions of liberty as the "only asylum from foreign and domestic troubles, and from state persecutions." By early fall, news of the protests had spread throughout the country.[4]

—

* They became even more famous later. John C. Calhoun of South Carolina used them to justify the nullification of the Tariffs of 1832 and 1833 during the Nullification Crisis. Compact theory, which Jefferson defined in his draft of the Kentucky Resolutions, was prevalent in the Southern states' resistance to the civil rights movement in the twentieth century. The resolutions have come to symbolize at best a way to protect speech from an oppressive national government and at worst a way to shield the institutions of slavery and segregation.

In addition to the numerous local meetings protesting the Alien and Sedition Acts, there was a vigorous pamphlet and newspaper war between opponents and supporters of the laws. The longer format of pamphlets meant that the authors could expand on the arguments made in congressional speeches or meeting resolutions, and they echoed the arguments made elsewhere. Both Democratic-Republican and Federalist polemicists stressed the theme of danger. The source of that danger was either the government if the writer was a Democratic-Republican, or France and its agents if a Federalist. Democratic-Republican writers stressed the dangers posed by all Federalist policies. In the essay that got him arrested for sedition, Thomas Cooper railed against all Federalist policies. In particular, he argued that a standing army made the government independent of the people. A large standing army "arms the partizans [sic] of Government, it disarms, it paralyzes their opponents. . . . not to defend themselves against invaders from without, but against the friends from within."[5] It was the potential use of the Army against the government's domestic enemies that worried Democratic-Republicans. Furthermore, Cooper warned, "The iron hand of power in every despotic government bears hard upon the patriot author—Faction, Sedition, Demagogue, Anarchy, Disorganizer—these are cant terms in use in every nation whose rulers are aggrandizing themselves at the expense of the people."[6] The rulers could easily use the excuse of security to protect their own power and not the nation's independence. The Alien and Sedition Acts were only one example of Federalist oppression.

Federalists tried again and again to explain the exact danger the United States faced from France, resident aliens, and most importantly from domestic opposition, especially the kind of opposition the Democratic-Republican Party mounted. Federalist writers attacked both France and resident aliens. While one Federalist characterized France as a "five headed monster," another declared that immigrants could only be safe in America because "every scoundrel convict is King!"[7] He warned Americans of how quickly disreputable aliens could disrupt their lives. Others focused on the dangers of opposition. Pennsylvania's Joseph Hopkinson went so far as to characterize opposition as a disease. The people were being duped "by the interested and criminal views of base and artful leaders," who would "excite vile and groundless jealousies against your Government, that being no longer supported by you, it can no longer give you protection; and that conscious the strength of America is invincible when united, seek its overthrow by disunion." The object of opposition was not to defend liberty or correct abuses of government, but "It is the overthrow of your government and constitution, it is the disorder and ruin of your country, it is your annihilation as a nation they seek."[8] The only way to cure America was to eliminate the source of the infection.

In response, Democratic-Republican writers stressed how Federalist policies endangered the Constitution and how they believed the First Amendment should be interpreted. Democratic-Republicans raised alarms that the Alien and Sedition Acts were Federalists' first experiment and surely more oppressive measures could be forthcoming. Jefferson issued the same warning in his anti–Alien and Sedition Acts resolutions. St. George Tucker, a Virginia jurist, asked, if Federalists could be so casual with aliens' rights, what would they do to citizens' rights? He warned that the Alien Friends Act converted the federal government into "a monster of despotism . . . Liberty will in a moment be utterly destroyed, its essence annihilated, and its very name forgotten, or buried in the gloomy dungeons of oppression."[9] George Hay, who defended James Thomson Callender in his sedition trial, reasoned, "if the freedom of the press is not to be abridged, and if no man can tell where freedom stops, and licentiousness begins . . . It follows, then, that no law can be made to restrain the licentiousness of the press." He concluded, "The Freedom of the press, therefore, means the total exemption of the press from any kind of legislative control, and consequently the sedition bill, which is an act of legislative control, is an abridgement of its liberty, and expressly forbidden by the constitution."[10] Hay's "An Essay on Liberty of the Press," which was first printed in the *Aurora* and then as a pamphlet, was a persuasive argument for the absolute freedom of the press. Hay contributed to the articulation of what would become a Democratic-Republican Party principle.

Federalists considered such absolute liberty to be as just as dangerous as Democratic-Republicans believed limits on the press were. In fact, Federalists believed the safest and best kind of freedom had limits. As Pennsylvania state judge Alexander Addison told a grand jury, "liberty without limit is licentiousness; and licentiousness is the worst kind of tyranny, a tyranny of all." Addison further explained that nothing mattered more than confidence, because without confidence there would be no liberty. The men who wished to deprive the government of confidence "deprive government of its authority; and government without authority is anarchy; and anarchy is the worst tyranny. No crime, therefore, is greater, than that of slander, which

diminishing the people's confidence in the government, diminishes their security, and destroys their liberty."[11] The First Amendment, as they interpreted
it, indeed allowed for such limitations. Virginia Federalist and at the time US
Attorney General Charles Lee made the distinction between regulation and
abridgement, the word used in the First Amendment. All the law did was to
regulate the press to prevent sedition; it did not abridge the freedom of the
press. He wrote that laws that "prohibit and restrain the latter [seditious-
ness], will always be found to affirm and preserve the former [freedom]."[12]
Federalists justified limits on the press and aliens as necessary to the security and independence of the nation as well as the preservation of liberty.
Democratic-Republicans rejected such restrictions, and continued to challenge Federalists' vision of a narrow role of the people.

—

With a seeming stalemate in the pamphlet war, and with public meeting and
petition campaigns not producing any immediate tangible results, Democratic-Republicans turned to the state legislatures. Acting through state legislatures offered another, safer, option for Democratic-Republicans. Unlike
individuals, legislative bodies could not be prosecuted under the Sedition Act
or any other law. As was the convention, members when speaking or acting
in their official capacities were protected by legislative privilege. State legislatures could thus argue that the laws were unconstitutional without the
risk of arrest, under which Jefferson, Madison, newspaper editors, and others operated. A state legislature could also offer a safer alternative to popular meetings by having lawfully elected bodies voice the people's displeasure
with the federal government rather than unruly, unelected, unrepresentative
meetings.[13]

   During summer and early fall 1798, Jefferson, Madison, and others con-
ferred over strategy. They were careful about where and with whom they met
and corresponded, especially after Jefferson was criticized for meeting with
Bache and others while in Philadelphia. Jefferson defended himself by arguing that he would always receive them because "they are men of abilities, and
of principles the most friendly to liberty & our present form of government."
Furthermore, Jefferson asserted, "I know my own principles to be pure, and
therefore am not ashamed of them. on the contrary I wish them known, &
therefore willingly express them to every one."[14] On this last point, Jefferson was not completely honest. But in the same season that Jefferson made
this declaration, he hid his participation in one of the most famous protests

against the Alien and Sedition Acts—the Kentucky Resolutions of 1798. Jefferson wrote his draft of the resolutions in early fall of 1798 and probably discussed it with Madison during a few short visits. He purposely wrote only a handful of letters during the summer and fall of 1798 because of concerns that the post office, populated by Federalist appointees, would not keep his correspondence private. Jefferson could not and would not trust the federal post office.[15]

Although the Kentucky legislature did not pass the resolutions quite as Jefferson had written them, it is worth closely examining Jefferson's draft.[16] In much of it, Jefferson reiterated in strong language the state compact theory and advocated the strict construction of the Constitution—all arguments that others had made previously. He argued that the Alien Friends and Sedition Acts were unconstitutional based on the Tenth and First Amendments; he brought up the slave-trade clause as evidence that Congress could not interfere with immigration; and he emphasized that aliens as people could not be denied the right to trial by jury and due process. In addition, he accused Federalists of violating the doctrine of separation of powers by transferring judicial powers to the executive in the Alien Friends Act. He answered the Federalist claim that the Alien and Sedition Acts were authorized under the general welfare and necessary and proper clauses of the Constitution by asserting that such an interpretation "goes to the destruction of all limits prescribed to their power by the Constitution: that the words meant by the instrument to be subsidiary only to the execution of limited powers, ought not to be so construed as themselves to give unlimited powers." Most of the resolutions contained some version of the phrase that the laws were "unauthoritative, void and of no force." Jefferson repeatedly proclaimed that a state had the authority and responsibility to nullify federal laws it deemed unconstitutional, otherwise known as nullification.

In his first and eighth resolutions, Jefferson explained why a state had the power of nullification. He opened his resolutions by pronouncing the Constitution to be a compact in which the states "delegated to that government certain definite powers, reserving, each State to itself, the residuary mass of right to their own self-government." When the general government assumed undelegated powers, as it did with the Alien and Sedition Acts, these acts are "unauthoritative, void, and of no force." As to why the state and not the federal courts could judge a law unconstitutional, Jefferson answered that the courts, as well as Congress and the executive branch, were creatures of the Constitution and not independent of it. No common judge existed, and therefore each state, as party to the compact whose existence did not depend upon the Constitution, "has an equal right to judge for itself" and to decide the proper remedy.

The eighth resolve expanded upon the ideas of the first. Jefferson valued the Union but defined it narrowly as "for specified national purposes, and particularly to those specified in their late federal compact, to be friendly to the peace, happiness and prosperity of all the States." When the general government claimed undelegated powers, the question was what remedy the states had to preserve their own governments. No one would question Jefferson's first remedy, which was a change by the people through elections, but his second—nullification—was inflammatory. Jefferson argued "that every State has a natural right in cases not within the compact (*casus non foederis,*) to nullify of their own authority all assumptions of power by others within their limits: that without this right, they would be under the dominion, absolute and unlimited, of whosoever might exercise this right of judgment for them." Furthermore, he warned that the Federalists might not be done. Aliens were easy prey as "the safest subject of the first experiment," and citizens had been targeted in the Sedition Act. Now Jefferson warned that these laws and similar laws in the future "unless arrested at the threshold, necessarily drive these States into revolution and blood." With that, Jefferson threatened armed rebellion and secession. Moreover, his last line warned of violent resistance to the laws by promising that each state would "take measures of its own for providing that neither these acts, nor any others of the General Government not plainly and intentionally authorized by the Constitution, shall be exercised within their respective territories"—a dire warning indeed.

Jefferson's message to Federalists and their friends was not just that these laws would bring about what they hoped to prevent, but also that Federalists needed to consider the way they governed. Jefferson's resolutions highlighted the differences between Democratic-Republicans and Federalists with regard to how they viewed the proper role of the people in a republic. Jefferson framed these issues in the language of confidence and jealousy. He declared, "confidence is everywhere the parent of despotism." Those who believed that it was best to govern "by the rod" held the mistaken belief that order and security could be a substitute for freedom. Whereas confidence bred danger, for Jefferson, "free government is founded in jealousy . . . it is jealousy and not confidence which prescribes limited constitutions, to bind down those whom we are obliged to trust with power." The Constitution's power lay in the limits it imposed upon confidence, or upon the people's trust in those who wielded power. Jefferson defined the relationship between the people and the government as based on consent not coercion, vigilance not unconditional trust.

The Kentucky legislature modified and softened Jefferson's language. Although it did use Jefferson's phrases of nullification—"unauthoritative, void, and of no force" and "altogether void and of no force"—it did not unilaterally nullify the Alien and Sedition Acts. Instead, Kentucky called on the other states to declare the laws unauthorized by the Constitution. The legislature entreated the state's representatives and senators to use their best endeavors to repeal the laws. While Kentucky avoided the most inflammatory of Jefferson's language, it largely adhered to his arguments.[17]

Madison's resolutions for the Virginia legislature were milder and more ambiguous than Jefferson's. In fact, Jefferson suggested adding that the Alien Friends and Sedition Acts were "not law, but utterly null, void, and of no force or effect" to Madison's draft.[18] This phrase would have brought the Virginia Resolutions more in line with Jefferson's version of the Kentucky Resolutions. It would have also clarified Madison's more ambiguous language about the proper remedy. Jefferson's amendment was not included in the final version.

In contrast to Jefferson, Madison began his resolutions with less confrontational language and instead vowed to defend the nation "against every aggression either foreign or domestic and support the government's warranted measures." He also expressed "a warm attachment" and "sincere affection" to the Union, which required the state to be vigilant of infractions. Instead of the language of nullification, Madison used the term "interposition," which he did not explicitly define. He also was ambiguous about his remedy. Although the resolutions ended by declaring the laws unconstitutional, they simply asked that the states take "the necessary and proper measures" for "maintaining the Authorities, Rights, and Liberties, referred to the States respectively, or to the people." It is clear that Madison did not consider that a state should take such action against the general government under just any circumstances—only in cases, like the present, "of a deliberate, palpable, and dangerous exercise of other powers, not granted by the said compact." In the resolutions, Madison noted that the laws could not be justified by any delegated power. Furthermore, the Sedition Act "ought to produce universal alarm, because it is leveled against that right of freely examining public characters and measures, and of free communication among the people thereon . . . the only effectual guardian of every other right." Here Madison expressed views similar to Jefferson's. Madison believed that the people's relationship with their elected officials should not be the subject of law. Madison predicted that the end result of Federalist policies would be an abandonment of republican government and the eventual replacement of it with "an absolute, or at best a mixed monarchy."[19] With the passages of these resolutions, the states entered into the wider debate about merits of the Alien and Sedition Acts.

—

Responses to the Virginia and Kentucky Resolutions ranged from terse to complex. Ten of the other fourteen states condemned either one or both of the states' resolutions. Maryland was the southernmost state to censure Virginia and Kentucky. In North Carolina, the lower house passed a resolution favoring the laws' repeal, but the state senate rejected it. Thus North Carolina did not formally weigh in on the controversy over the Virginia and Kentucky Resolutions.[20] Georgia agreed that the laws were unconstitutional but refused to endorse nullification. Tennessee called for the laws' repeal. The states that criticized the resolutions argued that Virginia and Kentucky violated the Constitution by declaring the Alien and Sedition Acts unconstitutional. These legislatures claimed that only the federal courts, not states, could rule on a law's constitutionality. State legislatures could only propose amendments to the Constitution. Delaware simply dismissed Virginia's action as "a very unjustifiable interference with the general government and constituted authorities of the U. States and of dangerous tendency, and therefore not a fit subject for the further consideration of the General Assembly." The New York senate declared that every measure that weakened confidence "has a tendency to destroy the usefulness of our public functionaries, and to excite jealousies equally hostile to rational liberty, and the principles of a good republican government." They labeled the Virginia and Kentucky Resolutions "inflammatory and pernicious."[21] Massachusetts passed the most comprehensive resolutions. Massachusetts argued that if Virginia persisted in its claim that states could declare federal laws unconstitutional and oppose federal laws, then "the Constitution would be reduced to a mere cypher—to form and pageantry of authority, without the energy and power." And so Virginia undermined the whole idea of union because, by declaring a law unconstitutional, states would make the people choose between the state and the nation. Throughout the resolutions and report, Massachusetts was careful never to claim the same authority that it argued Virginia had wrongly claimed.[22]

—

At the end of 1798, Federalists still seemed to have the support of the majority of the people. With the pleas from Virginia and Kentucky resoundingly rejected by other legislatures and the pamphlet war waging with no resolution, Democratic-Republicans fell back upon petitions to Congress as a way to prove Federalists wrong. Democratic-Republican congressional leaders, especially in communities near the capital of Philadelphia, redoubled efforts to produce petitions against the laws. These petitions asked Congress to repeal not only the Alien and Sedition Acts but also the measures expanding the military and increasing taxes. The House of Representatives generally did not ignore petitions, regardless of subject. More than thirty petitions, mostly from Pennsylvania and Virginia with a smattering from New York and Delaware, were presented throughout the short session that ended on March 3, 1799, as required by the Constitution. Significantly, unlike the previous session, when the vast majority of petitions condoned Federalists' policies, no petitions in support of the laws were presented. The number of signers was noted in the *Annals of the Congress of the United States*, the era's version of the *Congressional Record*, which was highly unusual. Democratic-Republicans wanted to prove that there was an upsurge of support among the people in favor of repeal. In one of his speeches, Pennsylvania Democratic-Republican Albert Gallatin noted that almost 18,000 freemen from the surrounding counties had signed petitions just in the past few weeks alone, implying that more signatures could have easily been gathered given more time.[23] Federalists had no time to launch their own petition drive to counter the Democratic-Republican efforts. Perhaps they believed that they already had the support of the people and firm control of the Congress and therefore had no reason to prove it.

Democratic-Republicans and Federalists accused each other of manipulating the people and misinterpreting the people's wishes. Gallatin faulted Federalists for fearing the people. Federalists refuted the charge by dismissing the idea that these petitions represented the true sense of the people. Federalist James Bayard, in his various speeches, repeatedly used the word "firebrands" to describe the laws' opponents, often reproaching Democratic-Republicans for wanting to create more of them. And whereas Democratic-Republicans often called the French danger imaginary, now Federalists called the support for repeal fanciful.

Federalists challenged Democratic-Republicans' claim that the petitions represented the true voice of the people. Eventually, the petitions were referred to a committee of four Federalists, chaired by dependable partisan Chauncey Goodrich of Connecticut, and one Democratic-Republican: John Nicholas of Virginia. As expected, the committee concluded that repeal was inexpedient and presented its report to the House on February 25, less than a week before the end of the session. In the report, the Federalist-majority committee presented a vigorous defense of the laws repeating much of the same arguments made previously. Significantly, the committee put the Alien and Sedition Acts into their broader context, arguing that the measures should be considered as part of a general system of defense "adapted to a crisis of extraordinary difficulty and danger"—a danger that they genuinely believed still existed. Hence they asked the people to trust their leaders. Finally, they proposed a series of resolutions declaring it inadvisable to repeal the Alien Friends Act, the Sedition Act, and the military measures passed during the last session of Congress.[24]

The debate on the resolutions was predictable. Because the committee report was printed and distributed throughout the United States as an official defense of the laws, Democratic-Republicans, knowing that the House's proceedings were regularly published in newspapers throughout the country, sought to counter the report by restating the arguments against the laws and summarizing the arguments made in the petitions in lengthy speeches on the House floor. Gallatin and Nicholas took on this task for the Alien and Sedition Acts, respectively. For the most part, neither presented any new arguments, but they made their arguments as succinct as possible. They focused on the consequences of Federalists' policies, that is, the dangers of a federal government with unlimited powers. Gallatin asserted that if the Alien Friends and Sedition Acts were left to stand, it would "destroy every limitation of the powers of Congress. It will follow that instead of being bound by any positive rule laid down by their charter, the discretion of Congress, a discretion to be governed by suspicions, alarms, popular clamor, private ambition, and by the views of fluctuating factions, will justify any measure they may please to adopt."[25]

Nicholas and other Democratic-Republicans raised concerns about Federalists' narrow interpretation of the First Amendment, which included protections for religion, assembly, and petition along with speech and the press. They argued that if the government could regulate one component of the First Amendment, it could place restrictions on the others, especially on the rights to assembly and petition. Democratic-Republicans had complained

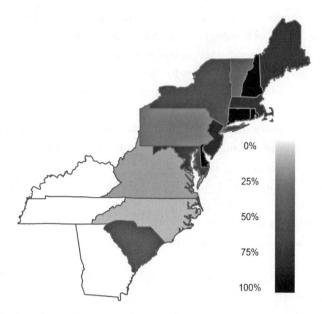

Support by state for the Alien and Sedition Acts as of February 25, 1799. On February 25, 1799, the House of Representatives passed two resolutions, by identical vote (52 to 48), declaring that it was inexpedient to repeal the Alien Friends and Sedition Acts. Thus a "yes" was a vote to sanction the laws. The map shows the relative support for the laws. Darker shading indicates that more of that state's representatives supported the laws. *Source: Journal of the House of Representatives* (5th Congress, 3rd Session), February 25, 1799

before about the chilling effect the Sedition Act could have on the right to petition. New York Representative Edward Livingston had introduced this issue during the debate about whether to refer a particular petition when he accused the majority of wanting to brand petitions libel, because then "the right of petitioning will be reduced to narrow ground indeed." Democratic-Republicans pointed out the larger ramifications of the law: it affected not only the press but other rights as well.[26]

These Democratic-Republican congressmen believed they had a chance, probably remote, of repealing the Alien Friends and Sedition Acts. After all, they lost by a margin of only four votes on every resolution. Jefferson reported to Madison on the "scandalous scene" in the House. The Federalist caucus decided that they would not participate in the debate and held conversations, coughed, and laughed—essentially loudly ignoring their colleagues—so much so that Jefferson surmised that the speakers must have had to shout in

Vote against repeal of the Alien Friends and Sedition Acts in the
House of Representatives, February 25, 1799

State	Yes	No	Abstention
Connecticut	8	0	0
Delaware	1	0	0
Georgia	0	1	1
Kentucky	0	2	0
Maryland	5	3	0
Massachusetts	10	3	0
New Hampshire	4	0	0
New Jersey	4	0	1
New York	6	4	0
North Carolina	1	7	2
Pennsylvania	4	8	1
Rhode Island	2	0	0
South Carolina	3	2	1
Tennessee	0	1	0
Vermont	1	1	0
Virginia	3	16	0
Total	52	48	6
Federalist	52	2	2
Democratic-Republican	0	46	4

Source: Journal of the House of Representatives (5th Congress, 3rd Session),
February 25, 1799
Note: The House of Representatives passed two resolutions, by identical
vote (52 to 48), declaring that it was inexpedient to repeal the Alien Friends
and Sedition Acts. This table shows the numerical breakdown of the vote
depicted in the accompanying map by state and party.

order to have been heard.[27] If the close vote in the House was any indication,
the country was indeed narrowly divided.

—

Perhaps what had given Gallatin the belief that Democratic-Republicans had
a chance to repeal the laws was not just the anti-Adams petitions but also
the promise of renewed negotiations with France. Despite what most Ultra
Federalists hoped for, communication had never really ceased between the
two countries. Soon after the failure of the first mission, the French foreign
minister reached out to American diplomats in Europe, assuring them that
France would respectfully receive any minister the United States sent. This
assurance seemed to allay at least the concerns of many moderate Federalists.
After some controversy, the Senate approved the new mission, and the envoys
sailed for France that October. With the possibility of peace, pro-war Federal-

ists lost the support of their less strident colleagues. They continued to argue that the French could not be trusted and that the best way to achieve peace was still preparation for war. Federalists won this argument with regard to the repeal of the Alien Friends and Sedition Acts in the House that winter, but the second mission to France produced permanent rifts within their party. After the fact, from his ambassadorship in Europe, John Quincy Adams, the president's son, expressed his understanding of the need for an external enemy. He told William Vans Murray, who had barely been confirmed as a member of the mission and whose work was almost rejected by the Senate, that "An external wound must sometimes be kept open to prevent the internal humors from destroying the body. Without a quarrel abroad the government would not have an army at hand to check projects of disunion and rebellion [at home]."[28]

Rebellion at home was a real concern early that spring, when resistance to the Direct Tax, enacted to pay for the nation's defense, seemed to verge on what Federalists considered to be insurrection. At the same time that Congress was considering repealing the Alien and Sedition Acts and the Senate was debating Adams's proposed new mission to France, northeastern Pennsylvanians, many of whom had previously supported the Federalist Party, refused to pay their taxes. This episode was called Fries's Rebellion, so named after one of the leaders—John Fries—and also known as the Hot Water War, because at least one woman threw hot water on a tax assessor. Since the summer of 1798, these Pennsylvanians had expressed their dislike for the whole Federalist program of defense. The most serious incident of their resistance occurred when a federal marshal arrested eighteen men and held them at a tavern while awaiting the trip to the federal district court in Philadelphia. Fries led a group of men to rescue these prisoners. Without any violence, Fries achieved his goal, after which the prisoners and their rescuers returned home. When the news reached Philadelphia, Federalists quickly connected the tax resisters in Pennsylvania to the radical revolutionaries in France. This link was precisely what Federalists had been warning Americans about for the last couple of years. A short few days later, Adams issued a proclamation directing the insurgents to end their "treasonable proceedings . . . to disperse and retire peaceably to their respective abodes." Adams believed that it was absolutely necessary "to call forth military force in order to suppress the combinations aforesaid and to cause the laws aforesaid to be duly executed."[29] Alexander Hamilton, who was officially second in command of the Army, advised the secretary of war against sending in too few troops. He stated, "it ought to appear like a *Hercules*, and inspire respect by the display of strength."[30] Following Hamilton's advice, filtered through his cabinet secretaries, Adams called out 2,000 militiamen to suppress the rebellion. The militia met with no resistance.[31]

Eventually, the district attorney brought thirty indictments: twenty-seven for conspiracy, rescue, and obstruction of process, and three for treason, including Fries. The first indictments were brought under the Sedition Act, which in addition to its prohibitions on the press outlawed combinations and conspiracies. In this instance, the Sedition Act was quite effective and appropriate. The treason charges were another matter altogether. Fries and his compatriots were tried and convicted twice. The first conviction was set aside because of juror misconduct. In the second trail, Associate Justice Samuel Chase, who had presided over the sedition trials of Thomas Cooper and James Callender, issued an opinion at the start of the trial broadly defining treason beyond that contained in the Constitution.* Fries's counsel resigned in protest. Consequently, Chase not only presided over the trial, but also served as Fries's counsel. The jury again convicted Fries.[32]

Some Federalists believed the convictions were a victory for order and a rejection of extralegal or extraconstitutional protests. Adams expressed his doubts that conviction would strengthen the people's support for his government. For Adams, a pardon could have done more to boost the people's confidence than an execution would have scared the people into obeying the law. Adams pardoned Fries forty-eight hours before his scheduled execution in May 1800. Within the Federalist Party, there was disagreement about how to treat this incident—as a real insurrection or a limited protest against a particular set of laws. If the first, it justified their harshest measures and confirmed Federalists' worst fears. If a limited protest, then Federalists' support was weakening. In his decision to pardon Fries and thus understand Fries's actions as protest and not treason, Adams distanced himself from the ultra wing of his party, as he had started to do when he proposed the second mission to France. Federalists were divided over how to respond to crises at home and abroad, and these schisms would affect the outcome of the election.

---

* The Constitution defines treason as "only in levying War against them, or in adhering to their Enemies, giving them Aid and Comfort. No Person shall be convicted of Treason unless on the Testimony of two Witnesses to the same overt Act, or on Confession in open Court" (Article III, Section 3).

Democratic-Republicans, on the other hand, tried their best to distance themselves from the unrest. Jefferson cautioned that "nothing could be so fatal" as violent action or rebellion, which "would check the progress of public opinion" toward the Democratic-Republican cause by giving the people reason to rally around the Federalist government. Insurrection, Jefferson continued, was "not the kind of opposition the American people will admit."[33] After Fries's second trial, Governor James Monroe reported to James Madison that the message had been received by Virginians that any "attempt to excite a hot water insurrection will fail."[34]

As they watched the events of the winter of 1798–99 unfold, Jefferson and Madison, from Philadelphia and Virginia, respectively, saw their arguments fail to sway political leaders and the people again and again, but Jefferson remained hopeful that the people would soon realize their previous error and return to true republican principles. Throughout January and February 1799, Jefferson wrote several letters in which he remarked upon the growing strength of their cause in the Middle States. As the Federalist senators divided over the second mission to France, Jefferson's hopes for Democratic-Republicans rose. Yet state after state condemned the Virginia and Kentucky Resolutions; House Democratic-Republicans failed to win repeal of the Alien Friends and Sedition Acts; pamphlets and newspaper articles supporting the acts continued to be printed; and arrests for sedition continued unabated. Jefferson and Madison had to decide whether and how to respond.

Jefferson urged his friends to take up their pens and promised that he would distribute their tracts to members of Congress to take home with them at the end of the session. Jefferson did not believe that Democratic-Republicans would triumph immediately. He wanted to get as much material as he could into his friends' hands during the winter and spring, because he believed the summer would be the best time for restoring republican soundness to the people. He entreated Madison, "Every man must lay his purse & pen under contribution."[35] Yet he also cautioned his correspondents to use only constitutional means of petition and election to achieve their goals and especially not to engage in violence, because "the appearance of an attack of force against the government would check the present current of the middle states & rally them round the government; whereas if suffered to go on it will press on to a reformation of abuses."[36] Violence, like Fries's Rebellion, would have only played into the Federalists' hands. To Madison, Jefferson suggested "Firmness on our part, but a passive firmness."[37] In May, Madison won election to the Virginia House of Delegates, and that same year Democratic-Republican Thomas McKean won the gubernatorial election in Pennsylvania—only two of a handful of bright spots in elections where Federalists overall gained seats at the expense of Democratic-Republicans.

Over summer 1799, Jefferson, Madison, and James Monroe, Virginia's governor, plotted their strategy for the upcoming state legislative sessions. The question was whether and how Virginia and Kentucky should respond to the rejection of their 1798 resolutions. In late August, Jefferson wrote to Madison outlining his strategy. He believed that Virginia and Kentucky should pursue the same track and not yield silently to the other state legislatures. First, they should refute the arguments of the other resolutions and the congressional report. Second, the new resolutions should firmly protest the violation of rights and assert the reservation of "the rights resulting to us from these palpable violations of the constitutional compact." If in the future the federal government disregarded "the limitations of the federal compact, meant to exercise powers over us to which we have never assented," the precedents would thus have already been established. Third, Jefferson recommended expressing affection for the Union and a promise "to wait with patience till those passions & delusions shall have passed over which the federal government have artfully & successfully excited to cover it's [sic] own abuses & to conceal it's [sic] designs." If change did not occur and the true principles of the federal compact were not respected, Jefferson went so far as to threaten secession, saying that they would "sever ourselves from that union we so much value, rather than give up the rights of self government which we have reserved, & in which alone we see liberty, safety, & happiness."[38] In a face-to-face meeting in September with Madison and Monroe, Madison prevailed upon Jefferson to moderate his calls for secession. In guidelines for Kentucky, Jefferson backed away from his earlier calls for secession and suggested much more conciliatory language for the third point by suggesting that not every error was cause for scission. Secession should be the last resort and not the first; as Jefferson wrote, "we should never think of separation but for repeated and enormous violations so these, when they occur, will be cause enough of themselves." Jefferson refused to prepare anything specific for the Kentucky legislature, as he had in 1798, so he could avoid suspicion of his involvement.[39] In late November, Jefferson imposed a gag upon himself because he knew "that a campaign of slander is now to open upon me."[40] If the Federalists were divided among themselves, Jefferson did not want to give them any reason to overcome those differences.

Kentucky legislators seemed reluctant to consider another resolution.[41] Nevertheless, they passed one in early December. The resolution noted that they had not changed their minds regarding the constitutionality of the Alien and Sedition Acts. The legislature focused on the censure and invective heaped upon the state for its actions. Kentucky insisted that it did not mean to disturb the Union's harmony but rather was "anxious only to escape the fangs of despotism," and they could not simply let their silence be construed as acquiescence in the arguments made by other states. After declaring its attachment to the Union, Kentucky reiterated its concept of union and what it thought the proper remedy for violations of the federal compact should be. The resolution unequivocally stated that the states "have the unquestionable right to judge of its infraction; and that a nullification, by those sovereignties, of all unauthorized acts done under colour of that instrument, is the rightful remedy." Furthermore, the Alien and Sedition Acts qualified as a palpable violation of the Constitution, and "it would consider a silent acquiescence as highly criminal."[42] Kentucky used even more strident language than in its resolutions passed the previous year.

—

In the Virginia House of Delegates, Madison took a different approach and sought to explain and justify Virginia's action. In the lengthy *Report of 1800*, Madison responded to the objections of the other states—especially a state's right to declare a law unconstitutional—restated the case against the Alien and Sedition Acts, and finally issued a detailed critique of the doctrine of a federal common law of crimes. The most controversial section of the document, and the only section changed by the Virginia House of Delegates, had to do with whether and in what sense the states were parties to the Constitution.[43] This issue struck directly at the heart of controversy about whether the states had the power to judge the constitutionality of a federal law, and if they did, whether it constituted unwarranted interference in federal authority. In the final report, Madison proclaimed that in the original 1798 resolutions, "states" meant "the people comprising those political societies, in their highest sovereign capacity." And thus, in this sense, the Constitution was submitted to the states, the states ratified it, and consequently the states were parties to the compact. Because the parties to a compact were the rightful judges of last resort, they must decide those questions that were of "sufficient magnitude to require their interposition." Madison asserted that not all laws or actions by the federal government were subject to a state's interposition. Interposition was reserved for occasions "deeply and essentially affecting the vital principles of their political system." In most ordinary situations, the judiciary could act as an effective check on the general government, but in extraordinary situations of "a *deliberate, palpable,* and *dangerous* nature," like the present one, a state could interpose, "arresting the progress of the *evil* of usurpation, and of maintaining the authorities, rights and liberties appertaining to the states, as parties to the constitution." The question was that if the states did not act, who would, especially in cases when all departments proved ineffective against dangerous infractions. In the case of the Alien and Sedition Acts, the judiciary proved to be no check upon the executive, and hence it was "the ultimate right of the parties to the constitution, to judge whether the compact has been dangerously violated."[44]

Furthermore, the consequence of letting the current usurpation of power by the federal government stand was to invite consolidation, whose ultimate result would be to turn the republic into a monarchy. If, as Federalists argued, the Alien and Sedition Acts were constitutional because of the power consequent to the common defense and general welfare clauses, the enumerated powers had no meaning or effect, Madison claimed. The outcome would be to increase the president's "sphere of discretion" and the "excessive augmentation of the offices, honors, and emoluments depending on executive will." The increase in executive patronage and prerogative would have then allowed the president to secure his reelection or the election of his chosen successor. By this series of events, the United States would have been transformed into a monarchy. Democratic-Republicans could already see this process starting with the large increase in the number of offices filled by the president in the military.

Madison then discussed the constitutionality of the Alien and Sedition Acts. He added his own interpretations to the arguments made during the previous year of public debate. With regard to the Alien Friends Act, he focused on the issue of foreigners' rights in the United States. Foreigners owed a temporary obedience to American laws and Constitution while in residence, and in return for that obedience they were entitled to protection. This argument was one of the most cogent statements of why aliens should receive a jury trial and enjoy other rights. Likewise, Madison addressed the principle of preventative justice—the principle that the Alien Friends Act violated by allowing the president to deport an alien upon only his own suspicion. The suspect alien had no chance to investigate the grounds of that suspicion or to avoid jail by posting bond and promising good behavior according to usual procedures. Federalists had claimed authority to pass the law based on the power of Congress to suppress insurrections, but Madison contended that the power to suppress insurrections did not mean the power to prevent all of them, because such a policy would lead to too great a chance that people's rights would be violated. This point led Madison directly to the Sedition Act. Madison was not willing to sacrifice rights for order at all costs. In this instance, individual rights were more valuable than order and security.

Madison restated the three reasons given in the original resolutions that the Sedition Act was unconstitutional. First, the law was not sanctioned by a power delegated to the federal government. Second, the power to punish seditious speech was expressly and positively forbidden by the First Amendment. And third, the law should "produce universal alarm" for the specific reason that "it is leveled against that right of freely examining public characters and measures, and of free communication thereon." He noted that during the time the law was in effect, there would be two elections for the House of Representatives and one for the presidency, which meant that incumbents would have the protection of the law and their challengers would risk prosecution just by pointing out differences with their opponents. These elections could not be between equals. Federalists tried to assure the public that the law was lenient because it only punished the intent to defame, but Madison, as others had, pointed out that punishing a writer or speaker's intent could not prevent pernicious influence of any article or speech. One could not punish intent without damaging the right to freely discuss public characters and measures. Just as the government could not prevent all insurrections, it could not prevent all seditious speech without trampling upon the fundamental principles of a republic. Some seditious speech had to be tolerated to preserve freedom. Free communication, whether between individuals or states, could not be circumscribed.

Most alarming, Madison wrote, was the Federalists' insistence that the Sedition Act was constitutional and acceptable because of common law. Madison claimed that Federalists' use of a doctrine of federal common law of crimes was novel and extravagant. He reviewed the history of America from colonial times through the ratification of the Constitution and found that no such doctrine did exist or could have existed. The evidence against such a doctrine was stronger with every change of government. If this precedent was allowed to stand, Madison contended, it would expand the scope of federal law as to render state courts and laws irrelevant and "overwhelm the residual sovereignty of the states." The Constitution in several places referred to "cases of law and equity," which applied to civil law and not criminal law, and so the common law of crimes was not part of the federal government's jurisdiction. About a week after passing the *Report of 1800*, the Virginia legislature passed a set of instructions to its US senators. One instruction was to oppose any law or measure "founded on, or recognising the principle lately advanced, 'that the common law of England is in force under the government of the United States,'" except when specifically authorized by the Constitution. These instructions, written by William Branch Giles, who had resigned from the US House of Representatives to serve in the Virginia House of Delegates, expounded upon the dangers of a federal common law. They explained, "It opens a new code of sanguinary criminal law, both obsolete and unknown, and either wholly rejected or essentially modified in almost all its parts by state institutions. It arrests or supersedes state jurisdiction, and innovates upon state laws."[45] Giles's resolutions expressed the Democratic-Republicans' deeply held fears of consolidation.

—

The debate over the Alien and Sedition Acts was spirited (sometimes mean-spirited) and vigorous. As the debate stretched over summer 1798 to the Election of 1800, the venues and tactics changed from the federal legislature to public meetings to the state legislatures, back to the federal legislature and then to state legislatures. Throughout, Democratic-Republicans and Federalists articulated their competing visions of the American Republic. Democratic-Republicans were willing to risk some order and security for freedom of the press and speech. Federalists were unwilling to make this sacrifice. They stubbornly insisted that the danger from France, aliens, and some citizens was simply too great a risk for the young nation. After the Senate confirmed Adams's nominees for a second mission to France, the Federalists lost their most potent argument of imminent danger. As the people watched Federalists vigorously enforce the laws while the danger from France seemed to fade away, Americans began to lose confidence in Federalists' leadership and thus in the government. So, while Federalists held onto their power in the 6th Congress, the people began to abandon them.

epilogue

A "REIGN OF WITCHES" was how Vice President Thomas Jefferson described Federalist rule, and he hoped that the people would quickly recover "their true sight, and . . . [restore] their government to its true principles."[1] Jefferson's prediction came true, as Democratic-Republicans triumphed in the Election of 1800. The Alien and Sedition Acts, especially the Sedition Act, were a significant factor in the elections. The laws provided a concrete example of the parties' different visions of the people's role in a republic. Democratic-Republicans wanted to restore what they believed to be the proper relationship between the government and the people—not dictated by law but determined by the people themselves. After the election, Federalists, soon to be in the opposition, attempted to renew the Sedition Act, demonstrating that they did not see the law as only an instrument to destroy the opposition but as essential to establishing the boundaries of appropriate political debate, which were necessary to preserve the nation's security. Once in power, Democratic-Republicans' commitment to freedom of the press was tested. Democratic-Republicans consistently argued that the First Amendment prohibited the federal government from passing any law regarding the press, but they never denied—and often encouraged—states to prosecute seditious libel. What emerged in the first part of the nineteenth century was an uncertain consensus about the meaning of the First Amendment and the proper role of the people in a republic.

—

Democratic-Republicans won the election as much as the Federalists lost it. Democratic-Republicans conducted a vigorous campaign that Federalists could not match. The extensive network of Democratic-Republican papers, which grew as the election approached and as a result of the Sedition Act, was crucial to the party's victory. The Sedition Act did not silence the most influential papers, like Philadelphia's *Aurora*, which continued to be published even after its editor was indicted for sedition and held in contempt by the Senate. Yet it was a close election, and Democratic-Republican leaders feared either a repeat of 1796 or a Jefferson presidency with an Adams vice presidency. Unlike their Federalist opponents, Democratic-Republicans united behind their candidates.

Internal divisions doomed the Federalists as much if not more than the innovative and modern political tactics the Democratic-Republicans employed. President John Adams had neutralized the Federalists' most potent reason for the Alien and Sedition Acts and the expansion of the military when he initiated a new mission to France. No matter how remote the chance for peace, just its possibility meant that France was no longer the threat it had seemed a couple years earlier. In addition, Adams's pardon of John Fries was another indication for many Federalists, including Timothy Pickering and others, that Adams was not fit for office. The final straw for Adams was when the Federalist caucus—a meeting of Federalist congressmen and officials in Philadelphia—nominated him and Charles Cotesworth Pinckney, who had been one of the envoys on the first mission to France, but did not designate a presidential nominee. The Federalist Party leadership did not endorse Adams's reelection to the presidency, a sign of Adams's weak support within his own party. After the caucus, Adams purged his cabinet by firing the secretaries of war and state. When firing Secretary of War James McHenry, Adams let his anger get the best of him by telling McHenry that Hamilton was "the greatest intriguant in the World—a man devoid of every moral principle—a Bastard." Adams proclaimed that Jefferson was "an infinitely better man" than Hamilton. He charged McHenry with being subservient to Hamilton, "who ruled Washington and would still rule if he could." Adams proclaimed that he would rather be Jefferson's vice president "than indebted to such a being as

Hamilton for the Presidency." He also added that Hamilton was the leader of the "British faction," as deep an insult as any that Adams could have made. Then Adams fired Pickering for both disloyalty and incompetence. These firings were cathartic events for Adams. For others, they only confirmed what they had already thought of him. The Speaker of the House, a Massachusetts Federalist, saw the firings as proof that Adams was a "weak & frantic old man."[2]

Hamilton could not leave Adams's accusations unanswered. He preferred Pinckney over Adams and plotted to put Pinckney ahead of Adams in the Electoral College. Perhaps in an effort to promote Pinckney's candidacy, but almost certainly in an effort to derail Adams's, Hamilton wrote a letter that was subsequently published as a pamphlet titled "Concerning the Public Conduct and Character of John Adams." Hamilton asserted that Adams was not qualified for office because he suffered from "extreme egotism," and was vain, unstable, and unpredictable. Hamilton also denied he was a leader of the British Party and defended his own intentions.[3] Despite insulting the president, Hamilton was not prosecuted for sedition even though some, mostly Democratic-Republican, newspapers did call for it. Boston's *Constitutional Telegraph* asked, "Will such a notorious character as Mr. Hamilton be allowed to abuse the President of the United States with impunity?"[4] In Connecticut, the New London *Bee* observed that Hamilton's pamphlet "contains the most gross and libellous charges against Mr. Adams."[5] Thomas Cooper, who had been released after serving six months for sedition, also called for Hamilton's arrest. In a public letter addressed to Hamilton, he asserted, "I have right to try the experiment, whether *Republicanism* is to be the victim of a law, which *Aristocracy* can break through with impunity."[6] Hamilton never answered Cooper and never had to answer for his pamphlet in a court of law. Prosecuting Hamilton for sedition would only have increased many Federalists' animosity toward Adams and exacerbated the existing divisions within the party.

After May 1800, few Federalist newspapers outside of New England actively campaigned for Adams, and Democratic-Republican papers shifted the focus of their opposition to either Hamilton or Federalist policies.[7] Adams blamed Federalist editors William Cobbett and John Fenno Jr., editors of *Porcupine's Gazette* and the *Gazette of the United States*, respectively. In September 1800, he commented that from the moment the second mission to France was announced, these editors "aided, countenanced, and encouraged by *soi-disant* Federalists in Boston, New York, and Philadelphia, have done more to shuffle the cards into the hands of the jacobin leaders, than all the acts of administration, and all the policy of opposition, from the commencement of government."[8] Adams could only watch as his support crumbled more as a result of Federalists' actions than of Democratic-Republicans'.

The Electoral College ballots were not officially opened by Congress until February 11, 1801. The result was a tie between Democratic-Republicans Thomas Jefferson and Aaron Burr, each with seventy-three votes; John Adams finished third with sixty-five votes. The Constitution provides, in the case of a tie or if no candidate receives a majority of the Electoral College, that the House of Representatives voting by state (and not individually) must choose a president from the top two candidates. In this case, the lame-duck, Federalist-majority House of Representatives chose between two Democratic-Republicans. Although everyone knew Democratic-Republicans designated Jefferson as the presidential candidate and Burr as vice president, this fact did not stop Federalists and even Burr from toying with the idea of making Burr president. After more than thirty ballots in which Jefferson always came up one short of a majority, the deadlock was finally broken on February 17, and Jefferson was elected president.

—

During the election crisis, some House Federalists proposed that the Sedition Act be extended for another two years beyond its March 3, 1801, expiration date. If the Sedition Act was purely a party measure to destroy the opposition, Federalists should have let the law die a quiet death. Yet some Federalists believed that a federal sedition law, particularly with its protection and the insistence of the centrality of the truth, was absolutely necessary for the nation's survival, regardless of who held power. Despite their recent experience, these Federalists believed the law was necessary to protect both the people and the government from malicious falsehoods.

Robert Goodloe Harper, a strong proponent for the law since he first championed it, vigorously defended the law as not restricting the press but as actually protecting its freedom. He wanted the law to protect him in case he was forced "by the imbecility or mistakes of any future Administration in this country, to commence an opposition against it; not a factious, profligate, and unprincipled opposition, founded on falsehood and misrepresentation . . . but a manly, dignified, candid and patriotic opposition . . . and resting on the basis of argument and truth." Harper continued that he wished "to be enabled, by this law, to go before a jury of my country, and say that what I have written is true. I wish to interpose this law between the freedom of discussion and the overbearing sway of that tyrannical spirit" of the Democratic-Republican Party. He wanted "this law as a shield." As before, Federalists relied on the argument that the Sedition Act improved common law. Harper voted for the renewal of a law that "mitigates the rigor of the common law in this respect, and protects the liberty of the press and of opinion, by enacting that the truth may be given in evidence on indictment for libels against the Government."[9] The law mitigated the dangers of falsehoods and the tendency, Federalists believed, of malicious speech to lead to rebellion and insurrection. Harper was in the minority of his party. Some of his colleagues were willing to concede that the law, although once expedient, was no longer necessary. Ultimately, the House rejected the renewal bill by four votes.

—

With the Election of 1800, Democratic-Republicans became the majority party. Governing, rather than being in opposition, would test their assumptions about the proper role of the people in a republic. Jefferson's First Inaugural Address, delivered on March 4, 1801, was both an attempt at reconciliation and a statement of his governing philosophy. He asserted that the people rejected restrictions on speech by citizens and aliens. While the will of the majority should prevail, Jefferson cautioned "that the minority possess equal rights, which equal law must protect, and to violate would be oppression." With that, he asked for a restoration of "harmony and affection." After all, Jefferson explained, "every difference of opinion is not a difference of principle . . . We are all republicans, we are all federalists." Americans shared the goal of union and independence, and thus perhaps their differences were not enough to dismantle the Union. Specifically, Jefferson promised "Equal and exact justice to all men, of whatever state or persuasion, religious or political." He explained his principles of good government, which meant an explicit rejection of Federalist policies. What preserved Americans' liberty and independence was "a jealous care of the right of election by the people—a mild and safe corrective of abuses which are lopped by the sword of revolution where peaceable remedies are unprovided." Moreover, Jefferson called for "the diffusion of information, and arraignment of all abuses at the bar of the public reason:— freedom of religion; freedom of the press; and freedom of person, under the protection of the Habeas Corpus:— and trial by juries impartially selected." Jefferson called for the restoration and expansive interpretation of the rights Democratic-Republicans believed Federalists had violated.[10]

Upon assuming the presidency and control of both houses of Congress, Democratic-Republicans did what they could to correct the wrongs they believed Federalists perpetuated during Adams's administration. Jefferson pardoned everyone who had been convicted under the Sedition Act. In 1809, Congress finally refunded their fines. Congress revised the Naturalization Act of 1798, relaxing the requirements for citizenship. The new naturalization law, which was enacted in 1802, reinstated the five-year residency requirement, reduced from fourteen. Significantly, Democratic-Republicans once again allowed both federal and state courts to process citizenship applications. They thus returned to joint control what the Federalists had made exclusively a federal responsibility. In the 1802 law, aliens were no longer required to register upon arrival. Democratic-Republicans dismantled the Federalists' system of surveillance. In 1804, the Democratic-Republican Congress passed a law allowing those immigrants who had arrived between 1798 and the passage of the 1802 law to become citizens immediately instead of waiting the fourteen years required under the 1798 law. Until after the Civil War, the federal government ceded most control over citizenship to the states. Once again, the federal government established the requirements for citizenship and left the determination of the rights, privileges, and obligations of citizenship to the individual states.[11] Over the course of Jefferson's first term, Democratic-Republicans also abolished much of the Federalist system of defense and repealed the taxes needed to pay for it.

Although through his words and his actions Jefferson seemed to endorse absolute freedom of the press, he did not fully trust the press. Jefferson maintained, as he had in 1798, that a federal sedition law was unconstitutional but that states were not barred from placing restrictions on the press. In 1802, Jefferson was willing to conduct what he called an "experiment" of prohibiting federal government prosecutions for libel. By using this term, Jefferson implied that he would abandon unfettered speech if it did not serve the interests of the Union. He counseled, "Patience and well doing, instead of punishment, if it can be found sufficiently efficacious, would be a happy change in the instruments of government."[12] A year later, however, his faith wavered. Pennsylvania Governor Thomas McKean informed Jefferson of "infamous & seditious libels," which appeared daily and had "become intolerable." McKean recommended that these editors could "be greatly checked by a few prosecutions." He hesitated only because the papers generally attacked federal officials and requested Jefferson's "advice & consent" on the matter, as "This vice is become a national one, and calls aloud for redress." Jefferson responded quickly, agreeing with McKean that the papers contained so many lies that "even the least informed of the people have learnt that nothing in a newspaper is to be believed." In order to restore newspapers to their former credibility, Jefferson "thought that a few prosecutions of the most prominent offenders would have a wholesome effect in restoring the integrity of the presses. Not a general prosecution: but a selected one." He helpfully enclosed a paper of which he believed should be made an example.[13] Five months later, in summer 1803, Pennsylvania indicted Joseph Dennie, editor of the *Port Folio,* for seditious libel. He was not indicted for insulting the president, which he did often and with great skill, but for a piece against the spread of democracy. His case was postponed several times, and Dennie was eventually acquitted.[14]

Without a federal law, states became and remained the focus of sedition prosecutions. An 1804 New York seditious libel case, in which Alexander Hamilton played a crucial role, established a strong legal and legislative precedent that was adopted by many other states before the Civil War. Harry Croswell edited *The Wasp*—a Federalist paper—and was charged with seditious libel under common law for criticizing Jefferson. Following common law, the judge ruled that truth could not be presented as a defense. Indeed, he instructed the jury that they could only decide the fact of publication, and the Democratic-Republican jury convicted Croswell. Hamilton became involved with the case on appeal. In a six-hour, two-day argument before the state supreme court, Hamilton defined freedom of the press and the relationship between the people and the government somewhere between the Sedition Act of 1798 and the common-law doctrine of seditious libel. Hamilton asserted that "The Liberty of the press consists in the right to publish with impunity Truth with good motives, for justifiable ends though reflecting on Govt, Magistracy or Individuals."[15] The defendant had to prove both the truth of his statements and his good intentions. It was malice that made any writing—truthful or not—criminal. Libels and falsehoods could lead to disorder. Before 1800, Hamilton had stressed the importance of the people's confidence in the government and the dangers of the press undermining this confidence; after 1800, Hamilton adopted the Democratic-Republicans' language of vigilance. He stated that the purpose of the press was to guard against usurpations and abuses of power. As his co-counsel stated, the freedom of the press and discussion, with the sanction of the truth, was "essential to liberties of our country, and enabled the people to select their rulers with discretion, and to judge correctly of their merits."[16] Hamilton thus urged the court to accept truth as a defense and to consider the intent of the writer when deciding whether the accused was guilty of seditious libel. In addition, he asserted that it was the jury who should decide these questions of both fact and law. Hamilton's speech was a cogent argument for vigilance and jealousy, and against blind confidence in the government. In the end, the court evenly split, the prosecutors did not move for a judgment, and Croswell did not receive a new trial.

Even though Croswell was never given a chance to fully clear his name, the New York legislature took note of the trial and Hamilton's arguments in defense of Croswell. Less than a year later, in 1805, New York passed a sedition law using Hamilton's criteria: truth and good motives. The New York law became the model for many other states before the Civil War. It was more restrictive than the Sedition Act of 1798 because the defendant had to prove both good motives and justifiable ends, but it was more lenient than common law because the defendant could use truth as his defense. It established the criteria for seditious libel prosecutions in a republic. The law embodied and tried to resolve the contradictions in Americans' thinking about the issue.[17]

For Jefferson, these cases may have been instructive of the shortcomings of state proceedings against seditious libel. State seditious libel prosecutions had not stopped newspapers from attacking him or his policies. Jefferson's disappointment with the press grew over the course of his first term, so much that in his Second Inaugural Address he could no longer keep quiet. While he praised the people for choosing their representatives wisely and the representatives for following public opinion, he criticized the press and chastised the states for not enforcing their own laws. For Jefferson, his experiment had failed. If the press confined itself to the truth, then Jefferson believed it needed no restraint, but the press had not. He questioned "whether freedom of discussion, unaided by power, is not sufficient for the propagation and protection of truth—whether a government, conducting itself in the true spirit of its constitution, with zeal and purity, and doing no act which it would be unwilling the whole world would witness, can be written down by falsehood and defamation." All these abuses could have been corrected "by the wholesome punishments reserved and provided by the laws of several states against falsehood and defamation; but public duties more urgent press on the time of public servants, and the offenders have therefore been left to find their punishment in public indignation."[18] Jefferson believed that the people were not meting out this needed punishment. If the press truly served the public good, it would cultivate peace, protect liberty, and preserve law and order. At that moment, Jefferson did not seem to believe the press was serving this purpose. The issue of the existence of a federal common law was not settled until 1812 as an outgrowth of sedition cases prosecuted while Jefferson was president. The Supreme Court finally ruled that a federal common law of crimes did not exist.[19]

Significantly, during the War of 1812, President James Madison resisted efforts to enact a federal sedition law or to use state laws to silence the disloyal antiwar voices in New England. Instead, Madison preferred personal civil suits as the proper recourse an offended official should follow, a decision that the Supreme Court would reach in the 1964 case *The New York Times v. Sullivan*. While Madison kept a careful watch over New Englanders, none were ever prosecuted for sedition or treason during the war. Throughout the war, he remained optimistic that "the wicked project of destroying the Union of the States is defeating itself."[20]

As these last examples show, Federalist and Democratic-Republican views, with the exception of Madison's, seemed to merge during the first decades of the nineteenth century, with an insistence on truth as an essential prerequisite for the freedom of the press. The expiration of the Sedition Act did not settle the issue. Instead, an uncertain and unstable consensus emerged in the early nineteenth century. The debate over the Alien and Sedition Acts of 1798 was only the first of many extensive debates on these issues. Responsibilities shifted to the states for both defining citizenship and seditious libel. Many states adopted laws similar to New York's sedition law, which allowed for truth as a defense but also required good intentions on behalf of the printer, writer, or speaker. Hamilton's definition became the standard by which libel was judged. With the Election of 1800, Americans had rejected the Federalists' vision of the proper role of the people in a republic. As the ultimate failure of the Alien and Sedition Acts showed, the federal government could not legislate the terms of its relationship with the people. Yet the Democratic-Republican ideal of absolute freedom of the press and an unregulated relationship did not triumph completely, either. As the Democratic-Republicans settled into national power and Federalists into a permanent and weak opposition, there was a shift in how each party treated the people and the press.

The lessons of the Alien and Sedition Acts of 1798 were not necessarily long-lasting. The circumstances surrounding the passage of those laws could lead—and have led—to similar measures being enacted once again. The debates over the Alien and Sedition Acts of 1798 were only the first of many about the relationship between the government and the people; they have been renewed regularly generation after generation.

Acknowledgments

There are many people to thank for reading all or some of this book and for useful and fruitful conversations about the Alien and Sedition Acts and politics in the Early American Republic. Marion Nelson and John Stagg read the whole manuscript. Those long coffees at the Virginia Museum of Fine Arts BEST café with Marion were incredibly helpful in getting me to think about this project in new ways, making a better book. John Stagg read two different versions of the manuscript, and his continued support has been very meaningful to me. The members of FLEA (Fall Line Early Americanists) provided many helpful comments on several chapters and a supportive community. A special thanks to FLEA member Brent Tarter, who read extra chapters in addition to the chapters I presented at FLEA meetings. Peter Onuf and Mark McGarvie read parts of the manuscript and offered the usual good advice. Alexander Wolman, Daniel Halperin, and Marcia Halperin read the whole manuscript. In addition to reading the manuscript, Alex prepared the map of the 1799 vote against repealing the laws, as well as countless other things for which I cannot even begin to thank him. Thanks are also due to the Department of History at the University of Richmond, especially Hugh West, for providing encouragement, support, and an office. I am grateful to Charles Hoffer and, at Johns Hopkins University Press, to Bob Brugger, an anonymous reader, as well as the editorial staff, who all helped me complete and improve this project.

Notes

Prologue

1. As quoted in David Waldstreicher, "Federalism, the Styles of Politics, and the Politics of Style," in *The Federalists Reconsidered*, ed. Doron Ben-Atar and Barbara Oberg (Charlottesville: University of Virginia Press, 1998), 113.

2. Jeffrey A. Smith, *Franklin and Bache: Envisioning the Enlightened Republic* (New York: Oxford University Press, 1990), 160.

3. Benjamin Franklin Bache, "Truth Will Out! The Foul Charges of the Tories against the Editor of the Aurora . . ." (Philadelphia, 1798).

4. Thomas Jefferson to James Madison, May 10, 1798, in *The Papers of Thomas Jefferson*, ed. Barbara Oberg (Princeton, NJ: Princeton University Press, 2003), 30:344.

5. John Adams to Thomas Jefferson, June 30, 1813, in *The Papers of Thomas Jefferson: Retirement Series*, ed. J. Jefferson Looney (Princeton, NJ: Princeton University Press, 2009), 6:253–56.

6. *The Herald of Liberty* (Washington, PA), May 29, 1798. These accounts appeared in several newspapers outside of Philadelphia.

7. Waldstreicher, "Federalism," 99–101; Jeffrey L. Pasley, *The First Presidential Contest: 1796 and the Founding of American Democracy* (Lawrence: University Press of Kansas, 2013), 88–91.

8. Kenneth Bowling, "'A Tub to the Whale': The Founding Fathers and Adoption of the Federal Bill of Rights," *Journal of the Early Republic* 8 (Autumn 1988): 223–51. On the lack of consensus about the meaning of the First Amendment, see Leonard Levy, *Emergence of a Free Press* (New York: Oxford University Press, 1985).

CHAPTER ONE: Governing a Republic

1. *National Gazette* (Philadelphia), April 2, 1792.

2. Merrill D. Peterson, "Thomas Jefferson," *American National Biography Online* (Oxford: Oxford University Press); Jeffrey L. Pasley, *The First Presidential Contest: The Election of 1796 and the Founding of American Democracy* (Lawrence: University of Kansas Press, 2013), 32–37.

3. Jack N. Rakove, *Declaring Rights: A Brief History with Documents* (New York: Bedford Books, 1998), 99–107; Gordon S. Wood, *Empire of Liberty* (New York: Oxford University Press, 2009), 61–62; Lance Banning, "James Madison," *American National Biography Online* (Oxford: Oxford University Press).

4. James Madison to Thomas Jefferson, October 17, 1788, and Thomas Jefferson to James Madison, March 15, 1789, in Rakove, *Declaring Rights,* 160–66.

5. Forest McDonald, "Alexander Hamilton," *American National Biography Online* (Oxford: Oxford University Press); Wood, *Empire of Liberty,* 89–91.

6. Mark Schmeller, "The Political Economy of Opinion: Public Credit and Concepts of Public Opinion in the Age of Federalism," *Journal of the Early Republic* 29 (Spring 2009): 35–61; James H. Read, *Power versus Liberty: Madison, Hamilton, Wilson, and Jefferson* (Charlottesville: University of Virginia Press, 2000); Colleen A. Sheehan, "Madison v. Hamilton: The Battle over Republicanism and the Role of Public Opinion," *American Political Science Review* 98 (August 2004): 405–24.

7. Jeffrey L. Pasley, *"The Tyranny of Printers": Newspaper Politics in the Early American Republic* (Charlottesville: University of Virginia Press, 2001), 48–78.

8. As quoted in Jeffrey A. Smith, *Franklin and Bache: Envisioning the Enlightened Republic* (New York: Oxford University Press, 1990), 137.

9. Jeffrey L. Pasley, "The Two National 'Gazettes': Newspapers and the Embodiment of American Political Parties," *Early American Literature* 35 (2000): 51–86.

10. Rachel Hope Cleves, *The Reign of Terror in America* (New York: Cambridge University Press, 2009), 58–103; Matthew Rainbow Hale, "On Their Tiptoes: Political Time and Newspapers during the Advent of the Radicalized French Revolution, 1792–1793," *Journal of the Early Republic* 29 (Summer 2009): 191–218; Simon P. Newman, *Parades and the Politics of the Street* (Philadelphia: University of Pennsylvania Press, 1997), 120–51.

11. Cleves, *Reign of Terror in America,* 94; Ashli White, *Encountering Revolution: Haiti and the Making of the Early Republic* (Baltimore: Johns Hopkins University Press, 2010).

12. Wood, *Empire of Liberty,* 185–89; James Roger Sharp, *American Politics in the Early Republic* (New Haven, CT: Yale University Press, 1993), 78–80; François Furstenberg, *When the United States Spoke French* (New York: Penguin Press, 2014), 44–53.

13. George Washington, "The Proclamation of Neutrality," April 22, 1793, in *The Papers of George Washington,* Presidential Series, ed. Christine Sternberg Patrick and John C. Pinheiro (Charlottesville: University of Virginia Press, 2005), 12:472–74.

14. Alexander Hamilton, "Pacificus," no. 1, June 29, 1793, and James Madison, "Helvidius," nos. 1 and 4, August 24 and September 14, 1793, in *Liberty and Order: The First American Party Struggle,* ed. Lance Banning (Indianapolis: Liberty Fund, 2004), 142–52.

15. Christopher J. Young, "Connecting the President and the People: Washington's Neutrality, Genet's Challenge, and Hamilton's Fight for Public Support," *Journal of the Early Republic* 31 (Fall 2011): 435–66; Wood, *Empire of Liberty,* 181–85; Sharp, *American Politics in the Early Republic,* 75–78.

16. Albrecht Koschnik, "The Democratic Societies of Philadelphia and the Limits of the American Public Sphere, circa 1793–1795," *William and Mary Quarterly,* 3rd ser., 58 (July 2001): 615–36; Wood, *Empire of Liberty,* 162–64, 185–89.

17. As quoted in Stanley Elkins and Eric McKitrick, *The Age of Federalism* (New York: Oxford University Press, 1995), 457.

18. Thomas P. Slaughter, *Whiskey Rebellion* (New York: Oxford University Press, 1986); Terry Bouton, *Taming Democracy* (New York: Oxford University Press, 2007), 216–43.

19. George Washington, "A Proclamation," August 7, 1794, in *Papers of George Washington*, 16:531–37.

20. Alexander Hamilton to George Washington, August 5, 1794, in *The Papers of Alexander Hamilton*, ed. Harold C. Syrett et al. (New York: Columbia University Press, 1961–87), 13:24–58.

21. Pasley, *First Presidential Contest*, 89.

22. George Washington, "Sixth Annual Message," November 19, 1794, American Presidency Project, University of California, Santa Barbara, http://www.presidency .ucsb.edu/ws/index.php?pid=29436&st=Washington&st1=.

23. "Proceedings in the House of Representatives on the President's Speech," November 24–27, 1794, in *Liberty and Order*, 179–85.

24. Thomas Jefferson to James Madison, December 28, 1794, in *The Papers of Thomas Jefferson*, ed. John Catanzariti (Princeton, NJ: Princeton University Press, 2000), 28:228–30; James Madison to James Monroe, December 4, 1794, in *Liberty and Order*, 185–86.

25. Koschnik, "Democratic Societies of Philadelphia," 127–28.

26. Sharp, *American Politics in the Early Republic*, 113–16; Wood, *Empire of Liberty*, 196–98.

27. Alfred F. Young, *The Democratic Republicans of New York* (Chapel Hill: University of North Carolina Press, 1967), 451.

28. Todd Estes, "Shaping the Politics of Public Opinion: Federalists and the Jay Treaty Debate," *Journal of the Early Republic* 20 (Fall 2000): 393–422; Sharp, *American Politics in the Early Republic*, 117–36.

29. Sharp, *American Politics in the Early Republic*, 135.

30. Elkins and McKitrick, *Age of Federalism*, 559–61.

31. George Washington, "Farewell Address," September 19, 1796, Avalon Project, Yale University Law School, http://avalon.law.yale.edu/18th_century/washing.asp.

32. Pasley, *First Presidential Contest*, 219–20.

CHAPTER TWO: Extreme Revolution, Vexing Immigration

1. Douglas Bradburn, *The Citizenship Revolution: Politics and the Creation of the American Union, 1794–1804* (Charlottesville: University of Virginia Press, 2009), 222, 216–17.

2. Ibid., 1–17.

3. Marilyn C. Baseler, *"Asylum for Mankind": America, 1607–1800* (Ithaca, NY: Cornell University Press, 1998), 254–55.

4. George Washington as quoted in Rogers M. Smith, "Constructing American

National Identity: Strategies of the Federalists," in *Federalists Reconsidered*, ed. Doron Ben-Atar and Barbara B. Oberg (Charlottesville: University of Virginia Press, 1998), 24.

5. Ibid., 36–37.

6. Edwin G. Burrows, "Albert Gallatin," *American National Biography Online* (Oxford: Oxford University Press); John C. Miller, *Crisis in Freedom: The Alien and Sedition Acts* (Boston: Little, Brown, 1951), 49–50; *Biographical Directory of the United States Congress*.

7. Bradburn, *Citizenship Revolution*, 103–5.

8. As quoted in Smith, "Constructing American National Identity," 37; Bradburn, *Citizenship Revolution*, 133–37; Ashli White, *Encountering Revolution: Haiti and the Making of the Early Republic* (Baltimore: Johns Hopkins University Press, 2010), 113–15.

9. Michael Durey, *Transatlantic Radicals and the Early American Republic* (Lawrence: University Press of Kansas, 1997), 4–11; David A. Wilson, *United Irishmen, United States* (Ithaca, NY: Cornell University Press, 1998), 2.

10. Miller, *Crisis in Freedom*, 42; Alexander DeConde, *The Quasi-War* (New York: Charles Scribner's Sons, 1966), 99.

11. François Furstenberg, *When the United States Spoke French* (New York: Penguin Press, 2014), 97.

12. Alfred F. Young, *The Democratic Republicans of New York* (Chapel Hill: University of North Carolina Press, 1967), 359–61; Miller, *Crisis in Freedom*, 42–43.

13. Dumas Malone, *Jefferson and the Rights of Man* (Boston: Little, Brown, 1951), 16; idem, *Jefferson and the Ordeal of Liberty* (Boston: Little, Brown, 1962), 236.

14. Furstenberg, *When the United States Spoke French*, 291–97.

15. James Morton Smith, *Freedom's Fetters* (Ithaca, NY: Cornell University Press, 1956), 160.

16. Malone, *Jefferson and the Ordeal of Liberty*, 386.

17. Rufus King to Timothy Pickering, September 13, 1798, in *The Life and Correspondence of Rufus King*, ed. Charles R. King (New York: Putnam and Sons, 1895), 2:411–14.

18. Bradburn, *Citizenship Revolution*, 225.

19. Douglas Bradburn, "'True Americans' and 'Hordes of Foreigners': Nationalism, Ethnicity and the Problem of Citizenship in the United States, 1789–1800," *Historical Reflections* 29 (Spring 2003): 39.

20. Wilson, *United Irishmen*, 1–11.

21. Seth Cotlar, "The Federalists' Transatlantic Cultural Offensive of 1798 and the Modernization of American Democratic Discourse," in *Beyond the Founders*, ed. Jeffrey L. Pasley et al. (Chapel Hill: University Press of North Carolina, 2004), 21–32.

22. Jeffrey L. Pasley, *The First Presidential Contest: 1796 and the Founding of American Democracy* (Lawrence: University Press of Kansas, 2013), 364–75.

23. James Madison to Thomas Jefferson, December 5, 1796, in *The Papers of James*

Madison, ed. J. C. A. Stagg et al. (Charlottesville: University of Virginia Press, Rotunda, 2010), 16:422–24.

24. William Pencak, "John Adams," *American National Biography Online* (Oxford: Oxford University Press); John Ferling, "President Adams and Congress in the Quasi-War Crisis," in *Neither Separate nor Equal: Congress in the 1790s*, ed. Kenneth R. Bowling and Donald R. Kennon (Athens: Ohio University Press for USCHS, 2000), 294–332.

25. Elkins and McKitrick, *Age of Federalism* (New York: Oxford University Press, 1993), 556–61.

26. DeConde, *Quasi-War*, 9.

27. John Adams, "Special Message to Congress," May 16, 1797, American Presidency Project, University of California, Santa Barbara, http://www.presidency.ucsb.edu/ws/index.php?pid=65636&st=Adams&st1=.

28. Ibid.

29. DeConde, *Quasi-War*, 30–35.

30. Thomas Jefferson to Edward Rutledge, June 24, 1797, in *The Papers of Thomas Jefferson*, ed. Barbara Oberg (Princeton, NJ: Princeton University Press, 2002), 29:456–57.

31. As quoted in Smith, *Freedom's Fetters*, 24.

32. As quoted in Miller, *Crisis in Freedom*, 42.

33. Elkins and McKitrick, *Age of Federalism*, 561–62 (quote on 562); on the XYZ Affair, see William Stinchcombe, *The XYZ Affair* (Westport, CT: Greenwood Press, 1980).

CHAPTER THREE: Partisan Solutions

1. John Adams, "Special Message to Congress," March 19, 1798, American Presidency Project, University of California, Santa Barbara, http://www.presidency.ucsb.edu/ws/index.php?pid=65650.

2. James Madison to Thomas Jefferson, April 2, 1797 [1798], in *The Papers of James Madison*, ed. David B. Mattern et al. (Charlottesville: University of Virginia Press, 1991), 17:104.

3. Thomas Jefferson to James Monroe, March 21, 1798, in *The Papers of Thomas Jefferson*, ed. Barbara Oberg (Princeton, NJ: Princeton University Press, 2003), 30:191.

4. All quotes from the congressional debates can be found in the *Annals of the Congress of the United States* (5th Congress, 2nd Session).

5. Seth Cotlar, "The Federalists' Transatlantic Cultural Offensive of 1798 and the Moderation of American Democratic Discourse," in *Beyond the Founders*, ed. Jeffrey L. Pasley et al. (Chapel Hill: University of North Carolina Press, 2004), 278–80; Thomas M. Ray, "'Not One Cent for Tribute': The Public Addresses and American Popular Reaction to the XYZ Affair, 1798–1799," *Journal of the Early Republic* 3 (1983):

389–412; *A Selection of Patriotic Addresses to the President* (Boston: John W. Folsom, 1798).

6. For a general discussion of these measures, see Alexander de Conde, *The Quasi War* (New York: Charles Scribner's Sons, 1966), 89–98; Stanley Elkins and Eric McKitrick, *The Age of Federalism* (New York: Oxford University Press, 1993), 581–607; Gordon Wood, *Empire of Liberty* (New York: Oxford University Press, 2009), 239–67.

7. See James Morton Smith, *Freedom's Fetters* (Ithaca, NY: Cornell University Press, 1956), 113, for the quote about Allen—biographical details about Allen, Harper, and Otis are found throughout; Joseph W. Cox, "Robert Goodloe Harper," and Evan Sheppard, "Harrison Gray Otis," *American National Biography Online* (Oxford: Oxford University Press); *Biographical Directory of the United States Congress*.

8. Edwin G. Burrows, "Albert Gallatin," and Alexander De Conde, "Edward Livingston," *American National Biography Online* (Oxford: Oxford University Press); John C. Miller, *Crisis in Freedom: The Alien and Sedition Acts* (Boston: Little, Brown, 1951), 49–50; *Biographical Directory of the United States Congress*.

9. Smith, *Freedom's Fetters*, 35–155, provides a good legislative history of each law; on the Naturalization Act, see Douglas Bradburn, *Citizenship Revolution* (Charlottesville: University of Virginia Press, 2009), 162–67.

10. As quoted in Smith, *Freedom's Fetters*, 53.

11. "James Lloyd," *Biographical Directory of the United States Congress*.

12. Smith, *Freedom's Fetters*, 107–8.

13. *Aurora* (Philadelphia), June 29, 1798.

14. Alexander Hamilton to Oliver Wolcott, Jr. [June 29, 1798], in *The Papers of Alexander Hamilton*, ed. Harold C. Syrett et al. (New York: Columbia University Press, 1974), 21:522–23.

15. Henry Tazewell to Thomas Jefferson, July 5, 1798, and Stevens T. Mason to Thomas Jefferson, July 6, 1798, in *Papers of Thomas Jefferson*, 30:440, 30:444; James Roger Sharp, *American Politics in the Early Republic* (New Haven, CT: Yale University Press, 1993), 178–80.

16. Smith, *Freedom's Fetters*, 109–10.

17. Henry Tazewell to Thomas Jefferson, July 5, 1798, in *Papers of Thomas Jefferson*, 30:440.

18. Paul Finkelman, ed., *A Brief Narrative of the Case and Tryal of John Peter Zenger* (New York: Bedford, 2010), 31–38.

19. Leonard Levy, *Emergence of a Free Press* (New York: Oxford University Press, 1985), 297–301.

CHAPTER FOUR: Self-Inflicted Wounds

1. Benjamin Franklin Bache, "Truth Will Out! The Foul Charges of the Tories against the Editor of the Aurora . . ." *Aurora* (Philadelphia, 1798).

2. Thomas Slaughter, "'The King of Crimes': Early American Treason Law, 1787–

1860," in *Launching the "Extended Republic": The Federalist Era*, ed. Ronald Hoffman and Peter J. Albert (Charlottesville: University of Virginia Press, 1996), 90.

3. James Morton Smith, *Freedom's Fetters* (Ithaca, NY: Cornell University Press, 1956), 184–87.

4. Geoffrey Stone, *Perilous Times: Free Speech in Wartime* (New York: W. W. Norton, 2004), 46.

5. Fisher Ames to Timothy Pickering, November 22, 1798, in *Works of Fisher Ames*, ed. Seth Ames (1854; reprint, Indianapolis: Liberty Classics, 1983), 2:1299.

6. Smith, *Freedom's Fetters*, 159–76; John C. Miller, *Crisis in Freedom: The Alien and Sedition Acts* (Boston: Little, Brown, 1951), 185–87; James Morton Smith, "The Enforcement of the Alien Friends Act of 1798," *Mississippi Valley Historical Review* 41 (June 1954): 85–104.

7. Gerald H. Clarfield, *Timothy Pickering and the American Republic* (Pittsburgh, PA: University of Pittsburgh Press, 1980).

8. Smith, *Freedom's Fetters*, 160–61.

9. John Adams to Pickering, October 16, 1798, in *The Works of John Adams*, ed. Charles Francis Adams (Boston: Little, Brown, 1853), 8:606–7.

10. Smith, *Freedom's Fretters*, 164–69.

11. Timothy Pickering to John Adams, August 1, 1799, in *Works of John Adams*, 9:6.

12. François Furstenberg, *When the United States Spoke French* (New York: Penguin Press, 2014), 359–65, 375.

13. *Porcupine's Gazette* (Philadelphia, PA), February 20 and 21, 1799.

14. Smith, "Enforcement of the Alien Friends Act," 102–3.

15. Adrienne Koch and Harry Ammon, "The Virginia and Kentucky Resolutions: An Episode in Jefferson and Madison's Defense of Civil Liberty," *William and Mary Quarterly*, 3rd ser., 5 (April 1948): 152–53; Smith, *Freedom's Fetters*, 95.

16. Petition to the General Assembly of Virginia [2 or 3 Nov 1798], in *The Papers of Thomas Jefferson*, ed. Barbara Oberg (Princeton, NJ: Princeton University Press, 2003), 30:571–75.

17. Smith, *Freedom's Fetters*, 200–204; Jeffrey L. Pasley, *Tyranny of Printers* (Charlottesville: University of Virginia Press, 2001), 98–102.

18. Smith, *Freedom's Fetters*, 204–18; Wilson, *United Irishmen, United States* (Ithaca, NY: Cornell University Press, 1998), 38–40, 49–50; Joseph I. Shulim, "John Daly Burk: Irish Revolutionist and American Patriot," *Transactions of the American Philosophical Society* 54 (1964): 1–60.

19. Miller, *Crisis in Freedom*, 385–90.

20. Aleine Austin, *Matthew Lyon: "New Man" of the Democratic Revolution, 1749–1822* (University Park: Pennsylvania State University Press, 1981).

21. Accounts of Lyon's trial can be found in Smith, *Freedom's Fetters*, 221–46; Stone, *Perilous Times*, 48–54.

22. Francis Wharton, *State Trials of the United States during the Administrations of Washington and Adams* (New York: Burt Franklin, 1970), 333–44. All quotes from the trial are from this source.

23. Matthew Lyon, "Colonel Lyon's Address to his Constituents . . . Vergennes Gaol, January 10, 1799" (New London: s.n., 1799).

24. As quoted in Smith, *Freedom's Fetters*, 246.

25. My discussion of Cooper's trial is based on ibid., 307–33; Stone, *Perilous Times*, 54–60; Peter Charles Hoffer, *The Free Press Crisis of 1800: Thomas Cooper's Trial for Seditious Libel* (Lawrence: University of Kansas Press, 2011), 73–112; Forrest K. Lehman, "'Seditious Libel' on Trial, Political Dissent on the Record: 'An Account of the Trial of Thomas Cooper' as Campaign Literature," *Pennsylvania Magazine of History and Biography* 132 (April 2008): 117–39.

26. Wharton reprinted Cooper's own account of the trial in his collection. See Thomas Cooper, "An Account of the Trial of Thomas Cooper . . . on a Charge of Libel against the President . . ." (Philadelphia: John Bioren, 1800); Wharton, *State Trials of the United States*, 659–81. All quotes from the trial are from Cooper's pamphlet.

27. Jane Shaffer Elsmere, *Justice Samuel Chase* (Muncie, IN: Janevar, 1980); Margaret Hornsell, "Samuel Chase," *American National Biography Online* (Oxford: Oxford University Press); Stone, *Perilous Times*, 58.

28. Smith, *Freedom's Fetters*, 319.

29. Stevens Thomson Mason to James Madison, April 23, 1800, in *The Papers of James Madison*, ed. David B. Mattern et al. (Charlottesville: University of Virginia Press, 1991), 17:382.

30. Cooper, "Preface," in "An Account of the Trial."

31. James Monroe to Thomas Jefferson, January 4, 1800, in *The Papers of Thomas Jefferson*, ed. Barbara Oberg (Princeton, NJ: Princeton University Press, 2004), 31:290.

32. Michael Durey, *"With the Hammer of Truth": James Thomson Callender and America's Early National Heroes* (Charlottesville: University of Virginia Press, 1990), 29.

33. Stone, *Perilous Times*, 61.

34. Durey, *"With the Hammer of Truth,"* 103.

35. Wharton, *State Trials of the United States*, 689.

36. My discussion of Callender's trial is based on Smith, *Freedom's Fetters*, 334–58; Stone, *Perilous Times*, 61–63; Durey, *"With the Hammer of Truth,"* 127–35; Wharton, *State Trials of the United States*, 688–721. All quotes from trial are from Wharton.

37. James Monroe to Thomas Jefferson, June 1, 1801, in *The Writings of James Monroe*, ed. Stanislaus Murray Hamilton (New York: Ames Press, 1969), 3:289.

38. Pasley, *Tyranny of Printers*, 176–95; Wilson, *United Irishmen*, esp. chaps. 1 and 2; John K. Alexander, "William Duane," *American National Biography Online* (Oxford: Oxford University Press).

39. Smith, *Freedom's Fetters*, 278–82; Wharton, *State Trials of the United States*, 345–91.

40. Timothy Pickering to John Adams, July 24, 1799, in *Works of John Adams*, 9:3–4.

41. John Adams to Pickering, August 1, 1799, in *Works of John Adams*, 9: 5.

42. Smith, *Freedom's Fetters*, 282–88; Stone, *Perilous Times*, 65; "Copy of Indictment. No. I. In the Circuit Court of the United States" (Philadelphia, 1799).

43. Smith, *Freedom's Fetters*, 288–300; Stone, *Perilous Times*, 65–66; quotes from "Senate Report of the Committee of Privileges on the Measures . . . 19th of February" (Philadelphia, 1800).

44. Smith, *Freedom's Fetters*, 359–73; Wharton, *State Trials of the United States*, 684–87.

45. Smith, *Freedom's Fetters*, 270–74.

46. My discussion of Frothingham's case is based on Smith, *Freedom's Fetters*, 399–415; Robert W. T. Martin, "Reforming Republicanism: Alexander Hamilton's Theory of Republican Citizenship and Press Liberty," *Journal of the Early Republic* 25 (Spring 2005): 39–41.

CHAPTER FIVE: Equal and Opposite Reaction

1. As reprinted in *Herald of Liberty* (Philadelphia), July 23, 1798.

2. Seth Cotlar, "The Federalists' Transatlantic Cultural Offensive of 1798 and the Moderation of American Democratic Discourse," in *Beyond the Founders*, ed. Jeffrey L. Pasley et al. (Chapel Hill: University of North Carolina Press, 2004), 274–99.

3. Jeffrey L. Pasley, *The Tyranny of Printers* (Charlottesville: University of Virginia Press, 2001), 126–27, 407–9.

4. Douglas Bradburn, "A Clamor in the Public Mind: Opposition to the Alien and Sedition Acts," *William and Mary Quarterly*, 3rd ser. 65 (July 2008): 567–74.

5. Thomas Cooper, "Political Essays" (Northumberland, PA: 1799).

6. Ibid.

7. Amos Stoddard, "An Oration . . . on the Fourth Day of July, 1799" (Portland, ME: 1799); Silas Lee, "An Oration, Delivered at Wiscasset . . . on the Fourth of July, 1799" (Wiscasset, MA: 1799).

8. Joseph Hopkinson, "What Is Our Situation? And What Are Our Prospects?" (Philadelphia, 1798).

9. St. George Tucker, "A Letter to a Member of Congress; Respecting the Alien and Sedition Laws" ([VA?], 1799).

10. George Hay, "An Essay on the Liberty of the Press . . . by Hortensius" (Philadelphia: *Aurora* Office, 1799).

11. Alexander Addison, "Liberty of Speech and of the Press. Charge to the Grand Juries . . ." ([1798?]).

12. "Virginiensis" [Charles Lee], "Defence of the Alien and Sedition Laws" (Philadelphia: John Fenno, 1798).

13. Robert W. T. Martin, *Government by Dissent* (New York: New York University Press, 2013), 140–42.

14. Thomas Jefferson to Samuel Smith, August 22, 1798, in *The Papers of Thomas Jefferson*, ed. Barbara Oberg (Princeton, NJ: Princeton University Press, 2003), 30:484–86.

15. The Virginia and Kentucky Resolutions have been widely discussed and analyzed. For example, see Adrienne Koch and Harry Ammon, "The Virginia and Ken-

tucky Resolutions: An Episode in Jefferson's and Madison's Defense of Civil Liberties," *William and Mary Quarterly*, 3rd ser., 5 (April 1948): 145–76; K. R. Constantine Gutzman, "The Virginia and Kentucky Resolutions Reconsidered," *Journal of Southern History*, 66 (August 2000): 473–96; John C. Miller, *Crisis in Freedom: The Alien and Sedition Acts* (Boston: Little, Brown, 1951), 169–81; Brian Steele, *Thomas Jefferson and American Nationhood* (New York: Cambridge University Press, 2012), 240–65.

16. Thomas Jefferson, "Draft of the Kentucky Resolutions of 1798," October 1798, in *Papers of Thomas Jefferson*, 30:543–49. All quotes are from this document.

17. Kentucky Resolutions, November 10, 1798 (Frankfort, KY: 1798).

18. Thomas Jefferson to Wilson Cary Nicholas, November 29, 1798, in *Papers of Thomas Jefferson*, 30:590.

19. James Madison, "Virginia Resolutions of 1798," December 21, 1798, in *The Papers of James Madison*, ed. David B. Mattern et al. (Charlottesville: University of Virginia Press, 1991), 17:185–91.

20. Miller, *Crisis in Freedom*, 178–79; Frank Maloy Anderson, "Contemporary Opinion of the Virginia and Kentucky Resolutions," *American Historical Review* 5 (1899–1900): 225–52.

21. The Virginia General Assembly collected and published the other states' responses in "The Communications of Several States on the Resolutions . . . Respecting the Alien and Sedition Laws" (Richmond: 1799).

22. "Report on the Virginia Resolutions, Relative to the Alien and Sedition Laws . . . Legislature of Massachusetts . . ." (Boston: 1799).

23. *Annals of the Congress of the United States* (5th Congress, 3rd Session, February 25, 1799), 2993.

24. Ibid., 2985–93.

25. Ibid., 2993–3002.

26. Ibid., 3002–14.

27. Thomas Jefferson to James Madison, February 26, 1799, in *Papers of James Madison*, 17:244.

28. John Quincy Adams to William Vans Murray, January 27, 1801, in *The Writings of John Quincy Adams*, ed. Worthington Chauncey Ford (New York: MacMillan, 1913), 2:494–95.

29. John Adams, "Proclamation 9: Law and Order in the Counties of Northampton, Montgomery, and Bucks in Pennsylvania," March 12, 1799, American Presidency Project, University of California, Santa Barbara, http://www.presidency.ucsb.edu/ws/index.php?pid=65676.

30. As quoted in Stanley Elkins and Eric McKitrick, *The Age of Federalism* (New York: Oxford University Press, 1993), 697.

31. Robert H. Churchill, "Popular Nullification, Fries' Rebellion, and the Waning of Radical Republicanism, 1798–1801," *Pennsylvania History* 67 (2000): 105–40.

32. Paul Douglas Newman, *Fries's Rebellion: The Enduring Struggle for the American Revolution* (Philadelphia: University of Pennsylvania Press, 2004), 165–80; Thomas Slaughter, "'The King of Crimes': Early American Treason Law, 1787–1860,"

in *Launching the "Extended Republic": The Federalist Era*, ed. Ronald Hoffman and Peter J. Albert (Charlottesville: University of Virginia Press, 1996), 95–108.

33. Thomas Jefferson to Edmund Pendleton, February 14, 1799, in *The Papers of Thomas Jefferson*, ed. Barbara Oberg (Princeton, NJ: Princeton University Press, 2004), 31:36–37.

34. James Monroe to James Madison, May 15, 1800, in *Papers of James Madison*, 17:388.

35. Thomas Jefferson to James Madison, February 5, 1799, in *Papers of James Madison*, 17:227.

36. Thomas Jefferson to Archibald Stuart, February 13, 1799, in *Papers of Thomas Jefferson*, 31:35.

37. Thomas Jefferson to James Madison, January 30, 1799, in *Papers of James Madison*, 17:223–24.

38. Thomas Jefferson to James Madison, August 23, 1799, in *Papers of James Madison*, 17:257–59.

39. Thomas Jefferson to Wilson Cary Nicholas, September 5, 1799, in *Papers of Thomas Jefferson*, 31:178–79.

40. Thomas Jefferson to John Taylor, November 26, 1799, in *Papers of Thomas Jefferson*, 31:244.

41. John Breckinridge to Thomas Jefferson, December 13, 1799, in *Papers of Thomas Jefferson*, 31:266–67.

42. "Kentucky Resolution of 1799," December 3, 1799, Avalon Project, Yale University Law School, http://avalon.law.yale.edu/18th_century/kenres.asp.

43. "Report of 1800: Editorial Note," in *Papers of James Madison*, 17:303–7. My discussion of the report is influenced by Leonard Levy, *Emergence of a Free Press* (New York: Oxford University Press, 1985), 315–25.

44. James Madison, "Report of 1800," in *Papers of James Madison*, 17:307–51. All quotes are from this document.

45. "Instructions to Virginia's Senators," Virginia House of Delegates, January 11, 1800, in *The Virginia Report of 1799–1800 Touching the Alien and Sedition Laws* . . . (Richmond: J. W. Randolph, 1850).

Epilogue

1. Thomas Jefferson to John Taylor, June 4, 1798, in *The Papers of Thomas Jefferson*, ed. Barbara Oberg (Princeton, NJ: Princeton University Press, 2003), 30:389.

2. Theodore Sedgwick to Alexander Hamilton, May 13, 1800, in *The Papers of Alexander Hamilton*, ed. Harold C. Syrett et al. (New York: Columbia University Press, 1961–87), 24:482.

3. Alexander Hamilton, "Letter from Alexander Hamilton, concerning the public conduct and character of John Adams, Esq. president of the United States" (New York, 1800).

4. *Constitutional Telegraph* (Boston), November 1, 1800.

5. *The Bee* (New London, CT), October 22, 1800.

6. *Philadelphia Gazette* (Philadelphia), November 19, 1800.

7. John Ferling, *Adams v. Jefferson: The Tumultuous Election of 1800* (New York: Oxford University Press, 2004), 150.

8. John Adams to John Trumbull, September 10, 1800, in *The Works of John Adams*, ed. Charles Francis Adams (Boston: Little, Brown, 1853), 9:83–84.

9. *Annals of the Congress of the United States* (6th Congress, 2nd Session, January 21, 1801), 940.

10. Thomas Jefferson, First Inaugural Address, March 4, 1801, in *Papers of Thomas Jefferson*, 33:148–52.

11. Douglas Bradburn, *The Citizenship Revolution: The Politics and the Creation of the American Union, 1774–1804* (Charlottesville: University of Virginia Press, 2009), 285–86.

12. Thomas Jefferson to Levi Lincoln, March 24, 1802, in *The Works of Thomas Jefferson*, federal ed., ed. Paul Leicester Ford (New York: G. P. Putnam's Sons, 1905), 9:358.

13. Thomas Jefferson to Thomas McKean, February 19, 1803, in *Works of Thomas Jefferson*, 9:451–52; Dumas Malone, *Jefferson: The President, The First Term 1801–1805* (Boston: Little, Brown, 1970), 227–30.

14. Malone, *Jefferson*, 230–31; Leonard Levy, *Emergence of a Free Press* (New York: Oxford University Press, 1985), 340–42.

15. Julius Goebel Jr., ed., *The Law Practice of Alexander Hamilton* (New York: Columbia University Press, 1964), 1:840.

16. William W. Van Ness as quoted in Morris D. Forkosch, "Freedom of the Press: Croswell's Case," *Fordham Law Review* 33 (1965): 434.

17. Levy, *Emergence of a Free Press*, 339–40.

18. Thomas Jefferson, Second Inaugural Address, March 4, 1805, Avalon Project, Yale University Law School, http://avalon.law.yale.edu/19th_century/jefinau2.asp; Malone, *Jefferson*, 234.

19. *The United States v. Hudson and Goodwin*, 7 Cranch 32 (1812), Constitution Society, http://www.constitution.org/ussc/007-032.htm.

20. James Madison to Mathew Carey, September 19, 1812, in *The Papers of James Madison Digital Edition*, ed. J. C. A. Stagg (Charlottesville: University of Virginia Press, Rotunda, 2010); J. C. A. Stagg, *Mr. Madison's War* (Princeton, NJ: Princeton University Press, 1983), 477–83, 259; Alan Taylor, *The Civil War of 1812* (New York: Alfred A. Knopf), 415–16, 421.

Suggested Further Reading

Classic books about the Alien and Sedition Acts include those by Leonard Levy, John C. Miller, and James Morton Smith. Levy focuses on the First Amendment and civil liberties; see *Legacy of Suppression* (Cambridge, MA: Belknap Press of Harvard University Press, 1960), *Jefferson and Civil Liberties: The Darker Side* (Cambridge, MA: Belknap Press of Harvard University Press, 1963), and *Emergence of a Free Press* (New York: Oxford University Press, 1985). Smith's *Freedom's Fetters* (Ithaca, NY: Cornell University Press, 1956) recounts in great detail the legislative histories of the laws and their enforcement. Smith, Miller (*Crisis in Freedom* [Boston: Little, Brown, 1951]), and others argue the Alien and Sedition Acts were a misguided effort by Federalists to destroy the Democratic-Republican Party. They tend to vilify the Federalists and praise the Democratic-Republicans. William J. Watkins Jr. also follows this model in *Reclaiming the American Revolution: The Kentucky and Virginia Resolutions and Their Legacy* (New York: Palgrave Macmillan, 2004), although he has an explicit and controversial present-day political agenda that influences how he interprets the historical record. Partisan imperatives alone cannot explain the controversy; Federalists and Democratic-Republicans were fighting over the meaning of the Constitution and the republic.

Recent work on the broader political culture of the 1790s has changed the focus from what happened in Congress to what happened in the streets and the press. These books and articles do not blame the Federalists for causing strife throughout the country or the demise of their party, but instead focus on the competing visions that the Federalist and Democratic-Republican Parties had for the new American Republic. See Seth Cotlar, "Federalists' Transatlantic Cultural Offensive of 1798," in *Beyond the Founders*, ed. Jeffrey L. Pasley et al. (Chapel Hill: University Press of North Carolina, 2004), 152–73, Joanne B. Freeman, "Explaining the Unexplainable: The Cultural Context of the Sedition Act," in *The Democratic Experiment*, ed. Meg Jacobs et al. (Princeton, NJ: Princeton University Press, 2003), 20–49, David Waldstreicher, *In the Midst of Perpetual Fetes* (Chapel Hill: University of North Carolina Press, 1997), and Douglas Bradburn, "A Clamor in the Public Mind: Opposition to the Alien and Sedition Acts," *William and Mary Quarterly*, 3rd ser., 65 (July 2008): 564–600 and *The Citizenship Revolution* (Charlottesville: University of Virginia Press, 2009). Other valuable and interesting sources on citizenship are Marilyn C. Baseler, *"Asylum for Mankind": America, 1607–1800* (Ithaca, NY: Cornell University Press, 1998), James H. Kettner, *The Development of American Citizenship, 1608–1870* (Chapel Hill: University of North Carolina Press, 1978), and Rogers M. Smith, *Civic Ideals: Conflicting Visions of Citizenship in U.S. History* (New Haven, CT: Yale University Press, 1997).

There are several good works on the Constitution and Americans' understanding of and relationship to it. For example, see Jack N. Rakove, *Original Meanings: Politics and Ideas in the Making of the Constitution* (New York: Alfred A. Knopf, 1996). Thomas Jefferson's understanding of this relationship and American nationhood receives excellent treatment in Brian Steele, *Thomas Jefferson and Nationhood* (New York: Cambridge University Press, 2012).

Several historians and political scientists have explored riots and violence in American politics. See, for example, William Pencak, Matthew Dennis, and Simon Newman, *Riot and Revelry in Early America* (University Park: Pennsylvania State University Press, 2002), and Paul A. Gilje, *The Road to Mobocracy* (Chapel Hill: University of North Carolina Press, 1987) and *Rioting in America* (Bloomington: Indiana University Press, 1996). See also Simon P. Newman, *Parades and the Politics of the Street* (Philadelphia: University of Pennsylvania Press, 1997) and David Waldstreicher, *In the Midst of Perpetual Fetes* (Chapel Hill: University of North Carolina Press, 1997). Political scientist Robert W. T. Martin has examined the role of dissent in the American Republic through his theory of dissentient democracy in *Government by Dissent: Protest, Resistance, and Radical Thought in the Early American Republic* (New York: New York University Press, 2013).

So much has been written about the Bill of Rights and the First Amendment in particular. There are a few excellent studies of this topic that pay significant and careful attention to the eighteenth and nineteenth centuries, including Michael Kent Curtis, *Free Speech, The People's Darling Privilege* (Durham, NC: Duke University Press, 2000); Donna Lee Dickerson, *The Course of Tolerance: Freedom of the Press in Nineteenth-Century America* (Westport, CT: Greenwood Press, 1990), Robert W. T. Martin, *The Free and Open Press: The Founding of American Democratic Press Liberty, 1640–1800* (New York: New York University Press, 2001), Norman L. Rosenberg, *Protecting the Best Men* (Chapel Hill: University of North Carolina Press, 1986), and Geoffrey R. Stone, *Perilous Times: Free Speech in Wartime* (New York: W. W. Norton, 2004).

General histories of this period are important for putting the Alien and Sedition Acts into the broader debates about the character and nature of the American Republic. Gordon Wood's *Empire of Liberty* (New York: Oxford University Press, 2009) is a history of 1789 to 1815. Norman K. Risjord, *Jefferson's America*, 2nd ed. (New York: Rowman & Littlefield, 2002) and Richard Buel Jr., *Securing the Revolution: Ideology in American Politics, 1789–1815* (Ithaca, NY: Cornell University Press, 1972) have longer chronological time frames. The 1790s are the focus of Stanley Elkins and Eric McKitrick, *The Age of Federalism* (New York: Oxford University Press, 1993), Jeffrey L. Pasley, *The First Presidential Contest: 1796 and the Founding of American Democracy* (Lawrence: University Press of Kansas, 2013), and James Roger Sharp, *American Politics in the Early Republic* (New Haven, CT: Yale University Press, 1993). Two classics about the XYZ Affair and the Quasi-War are William C. Stinchcombe, *The XYZ Affair*

(Westport, CT: Greenwood Press, 1980) and Alexander De Conde, *The Quasi-War: The Politics and Diplomacy of the Undeclared War with France, 1797–1801* (New York: Charles Scribner's Sons, 1966).

Several articles and books address specific events or controversies of the 1790s that highlight the differences between the parties and how each conceived of the role of the people in a republic. On the French and Haitian Revolutions in America, see Rachel Hope Cleves, *The Reign of Terror in America: Visions of Violence from Anti-Jacobinism to Antislavery* (New York: Cambridge University Press, 2009) and Matthew Rainbow Hale, "On Their Toes: Political Time and Newspapers during the Advent of the Radicalized French Revolution circa 1792–1793," *Journal the Early Republic* 29 (Summer 2009): 191–218. Ashli White has written an excellent book about Haiti and American politics titled *Encountering Revolution: Haiti and the Making of the Early Republic* (Baltimore: Johns Hopkins University Press, 2010). On the Neutrality Proclamation, see Christopher Young, "Connecting the President and the People: Washington's Neutrality, Genet's Challenge, and Hamilton's Fight for Public Support," *Journal of the Early Republic* 31 (Fall 2011): 435–66. On the Democratic-Republican Societies, see Albrecht Koschnik, "The Democratic Societies of Philadelphia and the Limits of the American Public Sphere, circa 1793–1795," *William and Mary Quarterly*, 3rd ser., 58 (July 2001): 615–36. On the Whiskey Rebellion, see Thomas P. Slaughter, *The Whiskey Rebellion: Frontier Epilogue to the American Revolution* (New York: Oxford University Press, 1986). For a discussion of post-Revolution politics in Pennsylvania, including examinations of the Whiskey and Fries's Rebellions, see Terry Bouton, *Taming Democracy: "The People," the Founders, and the Troubled Ending of the American Revolution* (New York: Oxford University Press, 2007). On the Jay Treaty, see Todd Estes, "Shaping the Politics of Public Opinion: The Federalists and the Jay Treaty Debate," *Journal of the Early Republic* 20 (Fall 2000): 393–422 and *The Jay Treaty Debate, Public Opinion, and the Evolution of Early American Political Culture* (Amherst: University of Massachusetts Press, 2006). There are several articles in *Federalists Reconsidered*, ed. Doron Ben-Atar and Barbara Oberg (Charlottesville: University of Virginia Press, 1998)—in particular the articles by Rogers M. Smith, David Waldstreicher, and Keith Arbour—that address issues of citizenship, Federalists' political style, and the press.

Other works highlighting the ideological and philosophical differences between the parties are Marc Schmeller, "The Political Economy of Opinion: Public Credit and Concepts of Public Opinion in the Age of Federalism," *Journal of the Early Republic* 29 (Spring 2009): 35–62, Colleen A. Sheehan, "Madison v. Hamilton: The Battle over Republicanism and the Role of Public Opinion," *American Political Science Review* 98 (August 2004): 405–24, and James H. Read, *Power versus Liberty: Madison, Hamilton, Wilson, and Jefferson* (Charlottesville: University of Virginia Press, 2000). On the development of the partisan press, see Jeffrey L. Pasley, *"The Tyranny of Printers": Newspapers Politics in the Early American Republic* (Charlottesville: University of Virginia Press, 2001). For a biography of Benjamin Franklin Bache, see Jeffrey A. Smith, *Franklin and Bache: Envisioning the Enlightened Republic* (New York: Oxford University Press, 1990).

The story of British and Irish radical immigrants to the United States and their political activities after they arrived is well told by Michael Durey, *Transatlantic Radicals and the Early American Republic* (Lawrence: University Press of Kansas, 1997) and David A. Wilson, *United Irishmen, United States: Immigrant Radicals in the Early Republic* (Ithaca, NY: Cornell University Press, 1998). Durey also has a biography of James Thomson Callender titled *With the Hammer of Truth: James Thomson Callender and America's Early National Heroes* (Charlottesville: University of Virginia Press, 1990). On the influence of radical democratic ideas in the United States, see Seth Cotlar, *Tom Paine's America: The Rise and Fall of Transatlantic Radicalism in the Early Republic* (Charlottesville: University of Virginia Press, 2011). On the activities, some of which were suspicious, and lives of French liberal aristocrats who spent a portion of the 1790s in the United States, including Talleyrand and Volney, see François Furstenberg's excellent book *When the United States Spoke French: Five Refugees Who Shaped a Nation* (New York: Penguin Press, 2014).

Several articles have been written specifically about the Virginia and Kentucky Resolutions. The seminal article was written by Adrienne Koch and Harry Ammon, "The Virginia and Kentucky Resolutions: An Episode in Jefferson's and Madison's Defense of Civil Liberties," *William and Mary Quarterly*, 3rd ser., 5 (April 1948), 145–76. See also K. R. Constantine Gutzman, "The Virginia and Kentucky Resolutions Reconsidered," *Journal of Southern History* 66 (August 2000): 473–96. Biographers of Thomas Jefferson and James Madison discuss this episode extensively. The editorial notes introducing the resolutions and Madison's *Report of 1800* in the modern documentary collections are also a good source. For reaction to the resolutions, see Frank Maloy Anderson, "Contemporary Opinion of the Virginia and Kentucky Resolutions," *American Historical Review* 5 (1899–1900): 225–52.

Secondary sources about enforcement of the laws are more plentiful for the Sedition Act than for the Alien Friends Act. In *Freedom's Fetters*, Smith examines enforcement of the Alien Friends Act and is one of the few to do so. An invaluable primary source for the sedition trials is Francis Wharton, *State Trial of the United States during the Administrations of Washington and Adams* (New York: Burt Franklin, 1849; reprint, 1970). Aleine Austin has written a biography of Matthew Lyon, *Matthew Lyon: "New Man" of the Democratic Revolution, 1749–1822* (University Park: Pennsylvania State University Press, 1981), in which she gives an account of his trial and aftermath. For accounts of Thomas Cooper's trial, see Peter Hoffer, *The Free Press Crisis of 1800: Thomas Cooper's Trial for Seditious Libel* (Lawrence: University Press of Kansas, 2011) and Forest Lehman, " 'Seditious Libel' on Trial, Political Dissent on the Record: 'An Account of the Trial of Thomas Cooper' as Campaign Literature," *Pennsylvania Magazine of History and Biography* 132 (April 2008): 117–39. On Hamilton and seditious libel before and after 1800, see Robert T. Martin, "Reforming Republicanism: Alexander Hamilton's Theory of Republican Citizenship and Press Liberty," *Journal of the Early Republic* 23 (Spring 2005): 21–46. Thomas Slaughter clearly explains the role of the judiciary in the 1790s in " 'The King of Crimes': Early American Treason Law, 1787–1860," in *Launching the "Extended Republic": The Federalist Era*, ed. Ronald Hoffman and Peter J. Albert (Charlottesville: University of Virginia Press, 1996), 54–135. For a book-length treatment of Fries's Rebellion, see Paul Douglas Newman, *Fries's Rebellion: The Enduring Struggle for the American Revolution* (Philadelphia: University of Pennsylvania Press, 2004).

Much has been written about the Election of 1800. There are many interesting articles in James Horn et al., eds., *The Revolution of 1800* (Charlottesville: University of Virginia Press, 2002). Book-length treatments of the election include John Ferling, *John. Adams v. Jefferson: The Tumultuous Election of 1800* (New York: Oxford University Press, 2004) and James Roger Sharp, *The Deadlocked Election of 1800: Jefferson, Burr, and the Union in the Balance* (Lawrence: University Press of Kansas, 2010). A good account of Harry Croswell's case can be found in Morris D. Forkosch, "Freedom of the Press: Croswell's Case," *Fordham Law Review* 33 (1965): 415–48, and Hamilton's speech and other documents can be found in Julius Goebel Jr., ed., *The Law Practice of Alexander Hamilton* (New York: Columbia University Press, 1964), 1:775–848. Dumas Malone devotes a chapter in each volume of his Jefferson biography on the presidency to Jefferson and sedition. See *Jefferson: The President, First Term, 1801–1805* (Boston: Little, Brown, 1970) and *Jefferson: The President, Second Term, 1805–1809* (Boston: Little, Brown, 1974). On the Hudson and Goodwin case, see Gary D. Rowe, "The Sound of Silence: *United States v. Hudson and Goodwin*, the Jeffersonian Ascendency and the Abolition of Federal Common Law of Crimes," *Yale Law Journal* 100 (January 1992): 919–48.

There are lots of primary source documents available, many of which are available online. Print collections include Jack N. Rakove, *Declaring Rights: A Brief History with Documents* (Boston: Bedford Books, 1998) and Lance Banning, ed., *Liberty and Order: The First American Party Struggle* (Indianapolis: Liberty Fund, 2004). In addition to these collections, there are the founders' papers projects and older printed editions of letters of the Founding Fathers and others, including Jefferson, Madison, Hamilton, John Adams, Albert Gallatin, Rufus King, Fisher Ames, James Monroe, and John Marshall. *Early American Imprints, Series 1 and 2*, which includes printed material from 1639 to 1819, is available by subscription through many libraries. *Early American Newspapers* is also a valuable source. Congressional records, including the *Annals of the Congress of the United States*, have been digitized and are searchable at the Library of Congress's "A Century of Lawmaking for a New Nation," available at http://memory.loc.gov/ammem/amlaw/. Yale University Law School's Avalon Project is also a good source for public documents, available at http://avalon.law.yale .edu/. The American Presidency Project at the University of California, Santa Barbara, is a searchable database of presidential papers, available at http://www .presidency.ucsb.edu/. The National Archives' Founders Online is a searchable database of the founders' papers, available at http://founders.archives.gov/.

Index

Adams, Abigail, 76

Adams, John, 3, 42; biography of, 41; and Election of 1796, 39; and Election of 1800, 121–23; and enforcement of Alien Friends Act, 74, 75–76; and enforcement of Sedition Act, 80, 81, 83–84, 85, 92–93, 94; and France, 37, 41–42, 43, 49, 111–12, 113, 121; and Fries's Rebellion, 112–14; responds to public, 1, 51–52

Adams, John Quincy, 112

Addison, Alexander, 102–3

Adet, Pierre, 36, 40, 76

Alien and Sedition Acts, 70–71, 75, 109–10; as defense measure, 54, 74; description of, 6, 7; opposition to, 100, 101, 107, 117. *See also* Democratic-Republican Party; Federalist Party; *individual laws*

Alien Enemies Act, 6, 56–57

Alien Friends Act, 6, 36, 57–61, 65, 70, 88, 91–92, 117–18; enforcement of, 6, 75–77, 93; and rights, 7, 58, 102, 117–18

aliens. *See* France: immigrants from; Great Britain: immigrants from; Ireland: immigrants from

Allen, John, 51, 53, 65–66, 67

Ames, Fisher, 23, 74

Argus (New York), 73, 95–96

aristocracy, 34, 41, 122. *See also* monarchy

Army, US, 43

Aurora (Philadelphia), 2, 13, 38, 94, 95; critical of Alien and Sedition Acts, 57, 61, 102; as Federalist target, 51, 65, 66, 98, 121; and Sedition Act, 73, 74, 91, 92–93, 97. *See also* Bache, Benjamin Franklin; Duane, William

Bache, Benjamin Franklin, 13, 43, 51, 97; attacked by Federalists, 1, 2, 72; critical of Federalists, 26, 72; death of, 38; and William

Duane, 38–39, 91; and Election of 1796, 40; indicted for seditious libel, 78–79; and partisan press, 13, 38–39. *See also Aurora*; Duane, William; newspapers

Baldwin, Luther, 94–95

Bayard, James, 63, 64, 108

Bee, The (New London, CT), 122

Bill of Rights, 6–7, 58. *See also* Constitution, US; First Amendment

Blount, William, 46

Burk, John Daly, 30, 37–38, 74, 79. *See also* Ireland: immigrants from

Burr, Aaron, 123

Cabell, Samuel J., 74, 77–78, 113

Callender, James Thomson, 39, 73, 74, 75, 87–91, 102

Chase, Samuel, 84–85, 86, 87, 88, 89–90, 113

circular letters, 67, 74

citizenship, 31–32, 34, 44–45, 54–55, 125; and US Constitution, 31

Cobbett, William (Peter Porcupine), 3, 77, 100, 122–23

Collot, Georges-Henri Victor, 36, 76–77

common law, 70, 124, 126–27, 128; definition of, 63, 75, 77; indictments for sedition under, 74, 77–80, 95–96; and James Madison, 116, 118–19

compact theory, 104–5, 106, 107, 116–17

Congress, US, 16, 33–34, 42–43, 44, 54, 83, 99, 123. *See also* House of Representatives, US; Senate, US

Constitution, US: common defense clause of, 59, 117; general welfare clause of, 59, 104, 117; rights in, 58, 104, 109–10, 117–18, 124–25; slave trade clause of, 58–59, 104; Tenth Amendment of, 58, 69, 104